Born of Water and the Spirit

Entering the Kingdom

By
Steven A. Carlson

GUARDIAN
PUBLISHING, LLC

Copyright © 2019, Steven A. Carlson
All Rights Reserved
ISBN: 978-0-9827915-7-8
Printed in the United States of America

This edition published in January 2019 in association with

Guardian Publishing, LLC
Holt, Michigan

guardianpublishingllc.com

All rights reserved. No part of this publication may be reproduced, stored in a retrieval system, or transmitted in any form or by any means – electronic, mechanical, photocopying, recording, or any other – except for brief quotations in printed reviews, without the prior written permission of the publisher.

All Scripture quotations, unless otherwise noted, are taken from the Holy Bible: New American Standard Version (NASB), Copyright © 2002. Used by permission of the Zondervan Corporation, all rights reserved.

Acknowledgements

I was raised in a Christian home and my father was a minister. I have been part of the church for as long as I can remember. Consequently, as a youth I spent much time in God's Word. About fifteen years ago, when a friend challenged my views on baptism, I decided to write my answer rather than waste time engaging in a verbal debate. That resulted in my first book titled *Baptism and the Battle for Souls*. That experience led me to author other books and has helped guide me to a more mature understanding of godly instruction. To a large degree that maturity can be attributed to various ministers of the gospel who have influenced me throughout the years.

This work is dedicated to two ministers who have been instrumental in shaping my view of God's Word. The first is my father, Elton Carlson. It was his teaching that initially guided me and for this I am most grateful. He deserves credit for many things, not the least of which is my understanding of the biblical plan of salvation. When I was born, he was solidly grounded in what Scripture has to say about the path to salvation thanks in large part to the mentoring he received from godly men. For this reason, I have never gotten caught up in the precarious and labored analyses of certain passages of Scripture offered by the modern-day evangelical community.

The second minister I would like to recognize is my brother, Timothy Carlson. His biblical insights have been an inspiration to me and have strongly influenced my approach to God's Word. Tim has often edited and critiqued my writings, consistently improving the quality of the work. The depth of his theological understanding has, no doubt, played a significant role in keeping me grounded solidly in apostolic doctrine.

I would like to thank my sister, Naomi Nash, along with Craig Gates, a missionary and friend, for their proofreading and recognize my son, Adam, for his exceptional editing work. I could not have done it without them. Finally, I am most grateful for my wife, Denise, and her patience in allowing me the time and freedom to put words to paper in a manner that hopefully makes a difference.

Preface

Few topics stir up debate in the religious community as quickly and as passionately as baptism. Volumes have been written on the subject over the past two thousand years, and particularly over the last five centuries. Since the Reformation Movement of the sixteenth century, doctrinal views about baptism have become varied and conflicting.

Some insist that submission to baptism is, without exception, essential to salvation, claiming that it is necessary to overcome original sin (a view that has led to the practice of infant baptism). Others teach that baptism is meant only for believers yet deny its necessity. Still others teach that baptism was intended only for the first century, and perhaps exclusively for the Jews of that time. Beyond these few, there are a host of other viewpoints that find their way into the debate. Since there can only be one truth concerning baptism – the biblical truth – it must be the case that most of these teachings about baptism also conflict with Scripture.

One passage that has served as a battleground for this discussion over the past few hundred years is found in the third chapter of John's gospel where Jesus spoke with a man by the name of Nicodemus. The text states that one must be "...born of water and the Spirit" to experience God's kingdom. Presumably this means that one must be baptized to know salvation. However, since Jesus' directive to Nicodemus challenges certain beliefs concerning baptism, the meaning of the conversation John recorded has become a source of contention. Employing numerous innovative strategies, a multitude of people have sought to eliminate baptism from the text. Here is the passage in question.

> [1]Now there was a man of the Pharisees, named Nicodemus, a ruler of the Jews; [2] this man came to Jesus by night and said to Him, "Rabbi, we know that You have come from God *as* a teacher; for no one can do these signs that You do unless God is with him." [3] Jesus answered and said to him, 'Truly, truly, I say to you, unless one is born again he cannot see the kingdom of God.' [4]Nicodemus said to Him, 'How can a man be born when he is old? He cannot enter a second time into his mother's womb and be born, can he?' [5] Jesus answered, 'Truly, truly, I say to you, unless one is born of water and

the Spirit he cannot enter into the kingdom of God. [6] That which is born of the flesh is flesh, and that which is born of the Spirit is spirit. [7] Do not be amazed that I said to you, 'You must be born again.' [8] The wind blows where it wishes and you hear the sound of it, but do not know where it comes from and where it is going; so is everyone who is born of the Spirit." (John 3: 1-8)

The teaching found in Scripture is not so fragile that it can be frustrated by the creativity of men. The assorted challenges to this text not only fall short of eliminating baptism from the narrative, but they are easily refuted when the written word – God's Word – is given honest consideration. As James Burton Coffman (1905-2006) put it:

> The persistent and ingenious efforts of people to shout baptism out of this passage are in vain, for there is no way it can be made to disappear.[1]

Before diving into the narrative, it might be beneficial to address an issue in the Greek text that is not readily evident in English translations. With very few exceptions, English Bible translations employ the wording "...born of water and the Spirit" (v. 5) in this passage where spirit (Gr. *pneuma*) is understood to be a reference to the Holy Spirit. However, some scholars have noted the fact that, in the original language, no definite article (Gr. *to* meaning *the*) precedes the word *spirit* in this verse. Generally, when the Holy Spirit is in view in the New Testament, *pneuma* is preceded by some form of *to* as a matter of identifying this member of the Godhead. Thomas Constable of Dallas Theological Seminary has made the following observation concerning the wording of the text:

> The English translators have inserted it to clarify their interpretation of 'spirit' (Gr. *pneuma*) as the Holy Spirit. A more literal translation would be simply 'born of water and spirit.'[2]

Given this look into the Greek language, it could be argued that the verse should read *born of water and spirit* where *spirit* (small 's') depicts the human spirit rather than the Holy Spirit. It appears to be a reasonable argument based strictly on the absence of the definite article, but there is more to consider.

---

[1] Coffman, James B., *Coffman's Commentaries on the Bible - John*, A.C.U Press, Abilene, TX, 1974, p. 84.
[2] Constable, Thomas, *Expository Notes of Dr. Thomas Constable*, https://www.studylight.org/commentaries/dcc/john-3.html, accessed June 15, 2017.

In the Apostle John's writings, when the Holy Spirit is mentioned, most of the time the Spirit is identified using the definite article (e.g., John 14: 26; 1 John 3: 24; 4: 2, 13; 5: 6, 8), but that is not always the case (e.g., John 1: 33; 20: 22). The same is true of other New Testament writers like Matthew and Paul. Therefore, the identity of *pneuma* in John 3: 5 must be determined through other measures.

The Greek word *ex (*sometimes *ek* or *ejk)*, which has been rendered *of* in most English translations, could more accurately be translated *out of* or *out from*. Rather than *born of water and spirit*, the text might rightfully read *born **out of** water and spirit*. G. R. Beasley-Murray (1916-2000), a Baptist theologian of considerable renown, preferred the translation "by water and Spirit,"[3] It can be determined from his rendering of the verse that Beasley-Murray understood water (Gr. *hudor*) and spirit as contributing to the transformation process.

The expression *of water and spirit* constitutes a prepositional phrase where both *water* and *spirit* identify with the preposition *of* (Gr. *ex*). This is confirmed in the original language where water and spirit appear in genitive case in this verse. Genitive case can be used in various ways. According to writingexplained.org: "the definition of genitive case is *the grammatical case used to show a thing's source, a trait or characteristic, or possession or ownership.*"[4]

It seems the most reasonable explanation is that water and spirit, as they are depicted here, serve as either the source or instrumentation of rebirth. This is in keeping with the idea of being born *out of* water and *out of* spirit. The following explanation appears on the website ntgreek.org:

> **Genitive of Source** - Sometimes the genitive case indicates the source from which the head noun is derived or depends. The word 'of' could instead be translated '*out of*', '*derived from*', or '*dependent on*'. This use is relatively rare; rather source is often shown with the preposition ejk used with the genitive case.[5]

This idea of source and/or instrumentation is found elsewhere in Scripture. The following verse from Luke demonstrates this. In a rebuke

---

[3] Beasley-Murray, G. R., *Baptism in the New Testament*, William B. Eerdman's Publishing Company, Grand Rapids, MI, 1973, pp 228-229.
[4] https://writingexplained.org/grammar-dictionary/genitive case, accessed June 28, 2017.
[5] https://www.ntgreek.org/learn_nt_greek/classify-genitive.htm, accessed December 16, 2018

of the Pharisees, Jesus identifies the heart as a source for both evil and good.

> The good man out of (ek) the good treasure of his heart brings forth what is good; and the evil *man* out of (ek) the evil *treasure* brings forth what is evil; for his mouth speaks from that which fills his heart. (Luke 6: 45)

In Jesus' words to Nicodemus, water and spirit are depicted as critical elements in bringing forth new life. The genitive case indicates that spirit, like water, is a contributor to the rebirth process rather than the recipient of the regenerated life that results. Given biblical teaching on baptism, it can be reasoned that *spirit* serves as the source of renewal and *water* as the instrument that is used by God to effect rebirth. Therefore, it is evident that Jesus is referencing the Holy Spirit in this instance.

In the ensuing verses, as Jesus discusses the Spirit, the definite article precedes *pneuma* with the lesson of verse 5 still in view. In fact, in verse 6, Jesus reiterates, using the words "born of the (tou) Spirit." It is the human spirit that is renewed *through* the work of the Holy Spirit (cf. Titus 3: 5). Consequently, the use of *the Spirit*, as opposed to *spirit*, is reasonable and appropriate in this context, explaining why it appears in English translations. With this explanation in view, this work will remain with those who recognize *pneuma* as a reference to the Holy Spirit in this verse.

The above observations concerning the wording of the session between Jesus and Nicodemus touch on an important matter that is foundational to biblical study. Men like Coffman, Constable, and Beasley-Murray have done their best to faithfully apply *hermeneutic principles* to draw their conclusions. What are hermeneutic principles (a.k.a., hermeneutics)? The term refers to the philosophy and methodology of textual interpretation. Generally, it is the science that uses linguistic standards to honor the author's intended meaning and is most often applied to biblical analysis.

Hermeneutics must be applied properly and consistently in order to be effective. One cannot disregard a principle of hermeneutics simply because it leads to an unwanted conclusion. The proper use of hermeneutics involves candidly examining the words of the text, appreciating the context of the passage (respecting how it fits into and is affected by both the immediate and expanded text), and recognizing the relationship between the characters in the narrative and the lesson(s) drawn from that narrative. This presumably helps one set aside personal doctrinal bias in determining an author's intended meaning in a passage of Scripture.

Honest application of hermeneutics will help render a meaning that complements the greater biblical landscape since interpretation of a specific passage must harmonize with the balance of Scripture. This harmony is such that other portions of Scripture often provide clarification when studying a given passage. The goal of this work is to apply hermeneutic principles to the conversation in question in a forthright manner in order to gain insight into the meaning of Jesus' words to Nicodemus and explore how that teaching affects the church generally.

Table of Contents

Title	Page
CHAPTER 1: THE NICODEMUS ENCOUNTER	11
The Pharisees	11
The Encounter	12
Born Again	13
Born of Water and the Spirit	13
Zwingli and Calvin	14
CHAPTER 2: BORN OF WATER - CHILDBIRTH	18
Covenant Childbirth	18
Birth and Rebirth	18
Flesh is Flesh	20
Unless One is Born Again	20
Two Elements of One Birth	21
CHAPTER 3: BORN OF WATER - GOD'S WORD	23
Water and the Word	23
The Old Testament	24
The New Testament	25
Logos vs. Rhema	26
CHAPTER 4: BORN OF WATER - THE HOLY SPIRIT	34
The Water/Spirit Connection	34
Even	36
Kai	39
The King James Bible	40
Exceptions to the Rule	42
Verb-Preposition-Noun-Kai-Noun	45
CHAPTER 5: BORN OF WATER - JOHN'S BAPTISM	49
The Design of John's Gospel	49
The Nature of John the Baptist's Ministry	51
The Nature of John's Baptism	53
John's Baptism and John 3	55
Born of God	59
CHAPTER 6: BORN OF WATER - CHRISTIAN BAPTISM	61
Introducing Christian Baptism	61
The Role of Christian Baptism	62

Title	Page

CHAPTER 6: BORN OF WATER - CHRISTIAN BAPTISM (CONT'D)

- AVAILABILITY OF CHRISTIAN BAPTISM 63
- MEN AND THEIR WORDS 65
- ENTERING THE KINGDOM 68
- THE NICODEMUS PERSPECTIVE 69

CHAPTER 7: BAPTISM IN CHURCH HISTORY 72

- BAPTISM AND THE EARLY CHURCH 72
- APOSTOLIC FATHERS 73
- ANTE-NICENE FATHERS 76
- NICENE AND POST-NICENE FATHERS 79
- THE PRE-REFORMATION PERSPECTIVE 81
- THE POST-REFORMATION SHIFT 83

CHAPTER 8: BAPTISM AND REGENERATION 85

- REGENERATION 85
- BAPTISMAL REGENERATION 86
- BAPTISM AND THE SPIRIT 87
- CHANGE OF STATE 90

CHAPTER 9: BAPTISM AS A SIGN OF SALVATION 94

- SEARCHING SCRIPTURE 94
- BAPTISM AS A SIGN 95
- BAPTISM AND CIRCUMCISION 95
- DEFINING A COVENANT SIGN 97

CHAPTER 10: BAPTISM AND NECESSITY 101

- BORN OF WATER 101
- ABSOLUTE NECESSITY 102
- RELATIVE NECESSITY 104
- RIGHTEOUSNESS AND GRACE 107

APPENDIX A 109

BIBLIOGRAPHY 110

Chapter 1

The Nicodemus Encounter

The Pharisees

The Pharisees were a peculiar sect. It is possible, and even probable, that the faction known as Pharisees began their mission altruistically. Religiously speaking, it is believed they may have derived their views from a segment of the Jews known as Hasideans who were recognized for their high regard for the Pentateuch and taught strict compliance with Judaic Laws.

The Jews of the Old Testament focused primarily on obedience to the law. The prophets had spoken and written of faith and circumcised hearts, but the law seemed more substantive and easier to understand. However, the Pharisees chose to teach the people not only to obey the law, but *how* to obey the law. It seems they believed the law did not speak well enough on its own behalf or the people were simply incapable of applying the law as the Pharisees saw fit.

The Pharisees developed certain rules for the Jews that were intended to complement the law. They insisted that by following their guidelines the people would be complying with the law. For instance, knowing the Sabbath Day belonged to the Lord as a day of rest (Exodus 20: 8), the Pharisees developed numerous rules designating what may or may not be done on that day. The claim was that godly expectations would be met if Pharisaic rules were obeyed.

Although the Pharisees' original intent may have been sincere, they began to drift away from godly principles prior to Jesus' birth. The rules they had developed began to replace God's law in the eyes of the Jews. These rules, often referred to as *oral tradition*, expanded to the point where even the most routine activities of the life of the everyday Jew were dictated by the Pharisees. By the time Jesus arrived, the Jews focused more on keeping Pharisaic rules than abiding by the law God had delivered to them. Most had come to believe that observance of these rules satisfied the legal minimums necessary to maintain their covenant relationship with God.

The high principles of the law (godliness and faithfulness) had been set aside in favor of keeping the letter of oral tradition leading to marked hypocrisy among the Pharisees as well as those who followed their teaching. It was the hypocrisy that disappointed Jesus and it was for this that he regularly challenged the Pharisees. He seemed to believe the Pharisees were in large part responsible for what he saw as a less than spiritual relationship between the Jews and their God.

The Encounter

The Apostle John, in the gospel letter that bears his name, offers a compelling narrative about an exchange between Jesus and a man by the name of Nicodemus. Two truths make the incident especially thought-provoking. The first of these truths is that Nicodemus was a Pharisee – the group with whom Jesus conflicted often in his ministry. Unlike most Pharisees, however, Nicodemus appears to have been religiously sincere. He recognized Jesus as having been sent from God and when he questioned Jesus, the narrative suggests a sense of candor.

Nicodemus approached Jesus at night, presumably because he did not want to have to deal with his cohorts among the Pharisees who would see him as a renegade. Upon meeting Jesus, he stated boldly, "Rabbi, we know that You have come from God as a teacher; for no one can do these signs that You do unless God is with him" (John 3: 2). A Pharisee acknowledging the fact that Jesus had been sent from God was unprecedented, and it is this statement that speaks to Nicodemus's honesty.

The second truth that makes Jesus' encounter with Nicodemus intriguing and even a bit controversial is that, during their conversation, Jesus spelled out at least a portion of what is necessary for one to be saved and attain eternal life. He told Nicodemus "Truly, truly, I say to you, unless one is born again he cannot see the kingdom of God" (John 3: 3). These words are compelling in that, with this remark, Jesus categorically laid down a tenet for salvation – a person must be *born again* to be a part of God's kingdom.

Born Again

It would be an epic challenge to find anything across the spectrum of creation that is more innocent than a newly born child. A newborn cannot do wrong since, at that stage of life, no sense of right and wrong exists. The innocent babe lives in a world of absolute purity – completely free from the concept of sin.

This is the idea of innocence that is in view in Jesus' words to Nicodemus. Becoming Christ's follower requires assuming a new, pure state, much like the innocent state of a newborn. This idea is represented with the words *born again*. It is a matter of becoming a new person, spiritually speaking. One who either fails or refuses to experience this spiritual rebirth cannot, according to Jesus' words, participate in God's kingdom.

The Greek terminology *gennethe anothen* is translated here as *born again*, which is how it appears in most English Bibles. It can mean either *begotten anew* or *begotten from above*. Many Bible scholars prefer the translation *from above*, insisting that it is more suited to the words, but given the discussion between Jesus and Nicodemus, *born again* seems to fit more comfortably with the narrative. For this reason, it is the commonly used English translation in this verse.

Perhaps the best understanding of *gennethe anothen* in this setting is to say that it means both *born again* and *born from above*. What Jesus revealed to Nicodemus was the spiritual regeneration (rebirth) of an individual. While regeneration occurs as one exists in physical (human) form, it is a spiritual birth that can only be occasioned by God, or *from above*. In other words, it is an earthly spiritual renewal.

Nicodemus's response to Jesus' words explains why the wording *born again* has been preferred over *born from above* in English translations over the centuries. The Pharisee asked Jesus, "How can a man be born when he is old? He cannot enter a second time into his mother's womb and be born, can he?" (John 3: 4). This response suggests that he was thinking strictly in human terms; hence the phrase *born again*. Still, the heart of his question was sincere. Nicodemus wanted to know how he could be reborn. If he could not see the kingdom without experiencing the rebirth of which Jesus spoke, knowing exactly what it involved was critical.

Born of Water and the Spirit

Jesus addressed Nicodemus's confusion by rephrasing his remark about seeing the kingdom. He responded in terms he believed would help the Pharisee understand what he meant by the expression "born again" (v. 3). Consider the following comparison of Jesus' statement and re-statement concerning rebirth.

> Truly, truly, I say to you, unless one is **born again** he cannot **see the kingdom of God**. (John 3: 3) – emphasis added

> Truly, truly, I say to you, unless one is **born of water and the Spirit** he cannot **enter into the kingdom of God**. (John 3: 5) – emphasis added

Jesus re-worded two specific phrases in a fashion that he knew would provide Nicodemus with the clarification he sought. The phrase *born again* has become *born of water and the Spirit*. This means that what Jesus intended with his phrasing of verse 3 is equally and fully present in the expression found in verse 5. The two utterances are being used interchangeably. Jesus used these words to explain to Nicodemus *how* he could be born again. Similarly, the phrase *see the kingdom* has been re-stated with the words *enter into the kingdom*. Thus, seeing the kingdom is another way of depicting participation in the kingdom.

Nicodemus had the answer to his question. He now understood how to be born again and it did not involve re-entering his mother's womb. As he had likely suspected, these words carried a spiritual meaning. He could now take full advantage of this information and seize his opportunity to partake in the kingdom of God.

The simple explanation is that Jesus was pointing Nicodemus to immersion in water (the rite of baptism) as it is taught in God's Word. The connection between baptism and the Spirit is found in the regenerating work of the Holy Spirit that occurs at the time of baptism (Titus 3: 5). Regeneration takes place during baptism as a person's old self dies to sin (confession and repentance) and is buried in the water (immersion/grave). At that time Christ's blood is applied as a spiritual cleansing agent (Acts 2: 38; 1 John 1: 7; Revelation 1: 5) removing the person's sins and, through the work of the Holy Spirit, a spiritually reborn individual rises from the water (Romans 6: 4).

Zwingli and Calvin

In Jesus' words to Nicodemus, baptism (born of water and the Spirit) is presented as a matter of salvation. This principle was applied in the first century as individuals were baptized for forgiveness of sins (Acts 2: 38; 22: 16) and, through baptism, realized newness of life (Romans 6: 1-4). However, Jesus' lesson to Nicodemus seems to have eluded many people beginning with the sixteenth century Reformation Movement.

Until the time of the Reformation Movement there was considerable unity among believers about the meaning of Jesus' words. He was identifying for Nicodemus the rite of water baptism that is portrayed in Scripture. In the sixteenth century, as the Reformers questioned the practices of the Roman Catholic Church, they began to identify baptism with other RCC teachings that constituted what they termed *works salvation*. At the forefront of the challenge to baptism were men like Huldrich Zwingli (1484-1531) and John Calvin (1509-1564). Zwingli even lauded himself as the first to understand that baptism lacked efficacy, stating:

> In this matter of baptism -- if I may be pardoned for saying it -- I can only conclude that all the doctors have been in error from the time of the apostles…for all the doctors have ascribed to the water a power which it does not have and the holy apostles did not teach.[6]

This declaration sparked the beginning of a dramatic shift in baptismal doctrine among the Reformers. Yet, even as men began to challenge the rite of baptism, they still did not question its necessity. When he wrote concerning Jesus' words to Nicodemus, Calvin made the following comments about how he believed the text should be understood.

> But though we were to admit that Christ here speaks of baptism, yet we ought not to press his words so closely as to imagine that he confines salvation to the outward sign; but, on the contrary, he connects the Water with the Spirit, because under that visible symbol he attests and seals that newness of life which God alone produces in us by his Spirit. It is true that, by neglecting baptism, we are excluded from salvation; and in this sense I acknowledge that it is necessary; but it is absurd to speak of the hope of salvation as confined to the sign. So far as relates to this passage, I cannot bring myself to believe that Christ speaks of baptism; for it would have been inappropriate.[7]

Calvin's rationale seems a bit inconsistent. On one hand, he appears to have understood Jesus' reference to the rite of baptism, but he believed that "…we ought not to press his words so closely that he confines salvation to the outward sign." In other words, Calvin believed

---

[6] Bromiley, G. W. editor and translator. *'Of Baptism,' in Zwingli and Bullinger, 'Library of Christian Classic" Ichthus Editions,* The Westminster Press, Philadelphia, PA, p. 130.
[7] Calvin, John, *Calvin's Commentaries,*
http://biblehub.com/commentaries/calvin/john/3.htm, accessed July 22, 2017.

that *even if* Jesus was pointing to baptism, which he questioned, men should not see his words as a proclamation of the necessity of baptism. Yet, contrary to his own argument, Calvin seemingly recognized baptism as a redemptive matter since, without it "…we are excluded from salvation."

In the end, Calvin insisted it would have been inappropriate for Jesus to make redemption reliant on submission to baptism since he considered it merely a sign of salvation. He saw nothing of true spiritual substance taking place within the ordinance itself. Therefore, while other Reformers may have embraced Jesus' depiction of baptism in his words to Nicodemus, Calvin refused to accept that interpretation of the text.

Calvin wrote during the early to mid-sixteenth century at the height of the Reformation Movement. His conflicting logic in the above paragraph is understandable since it was during this time that the debate over baptism began to surface. Calvin struggled heavily with the historical perspective that Jesus was instructing Nicodemus on the rite of baptism. He eventually came to deny that baptism was anything more than token obedience attesting to one's forgiveness. Still, he understood baptism as an "…initiatory sign by which we are admitted to the fellowship of the Church, that being ingrafted into Christ we may be accounted children of God."[8]

The debate over John 3: 5 centers on the meaning of the phrase *born of water*. Unlike Calvin, who struggled heartily with Jesus' words, modern-day evangelicals have enthusiastically abandoned the originally understood meaning of the text. They insist that Jesus could not have Christian baptism in view since this would portray the ordinance of water baptism as essential for entering God's kingdom – a teaching they have chosen to reject. In the modern age it is not a stretch to grant that most professed Bible scholars deny with utmost vigor any relationship between baptism and the water of this verse. A multitude of explanations have been offered and debated in connection with John 3: 3-5 over the past few centuries. Of the many that have been proposed, the following five doctrinal views seem to receive most of the attention.

---

[8] Calvin, John, *Institutes of the Christian Religion*, Hendrickson Publishers, Book Fourth, Peabody, MA, 2008, p. 859.

1. With the words *born of water and the Spirit*, two separate births are in view. It is said that *born of water* serves as a reference to physical childbirth while *born of the Spirit* identifies the spiritual rebirth one must experience to enter the kingdom of God.

2. The water of the text represents God's Word in a figurative sense. It is taught that God's Word, in cooperation with the Holy Spirit, offers the regeneration without which one cannot see the kingdom of God.

3. The Greek word *kai*, translated *and* in verse 5 (born of water *and* the Spirit), is at times translated into English using the word *even*. The claim is that Jesus was telling Nicodemus he must be born of water, *even* the Spirit. Such a rendering would mean that *water* and *Spirit* hold the same meaning and that *water* is simply another term for *Spirit*.

4. The expression *born of water* represents the water baptism performed by John the Baptist. This is a baptism that was performed only in the first century, but it is a baptism with which the Pharisee would have been familiar.

5. *Born of water* is representative of Christian baptism that was performed by the church on and after the Day of Pentecost and continues even today. Correspondingly, *born of the Spirit* depicts the combination of the regenerative work of the Holy Spirit that occurs during one's submission to Christian baptism and the *gift* (indwelling) of the Spirit that begins at that time.

While the baptism of John and Christian baptism both involve immersion in water, the other claims are antithetical. In other words, if one is true, the others cannot be true. What did Jesus mean by this statement? Since no one may enter the kingdom without experiencing birth of water and the Spirit, it is imperative that men understand it. The goal here is to examine Scripture and weigh the merits of each of these claims. Perhaps, by eliminating those without merit, the field of possibilities can be narrowed, and a determination can be made respecting the meaning of Jesus' words.

Chapter 2

- Born of Water -
Childbirth

Covenant Childbirth

When Jesus told Nicodemus, "…unless one is born again he cannot see the kingdom of God" (v. 3), the Pharisee heard these words from a Jewish/Pharisaic perspective. To Nicodemus, the Jews' relationship with God was grounded in childbirth. Every Jewish child, by the mere fact that he/she was born of Jewish parents, was a natural participant in God's covenant with Abraham and correspondingly one of God's chosen people. Birth was the means of entrance into that covenant.

His Jewish heritage helped Nicodemus understand the connection between childbirth and a covenant relationship, but what Jesus said about being born again seemed to confuse him. If he was already a participant in the Abrahamic covenant, why did he need to become part of what Jesus termed *the kingdom of God* and why would this require anything beyond his own natural birth of Jewish parents?

Birth and Rebirth

It was his understanding of the relationship between a Jew's physical birth and membership in the Abrahamic covenant that undoubtedly led to the Pharisee's follow-up question. Nicodemus's response appears to have been half-joking and half-serious as he asked, "How can a man be born when he is old? He cannot enter a second time into his mother's womb and be born, can he?" (v. 4). The question was rhetorical since Nicodemus knew Jesus would not suggest something so absurd. John MacArthur offers some excellent insight into Nicodemus's rather bizarre question stating:

> "Certainly, this highly educated Pharisee was not so obtuse as to have misinterpreted Jesus' words in a simplistically literal sense. He knew our Lord was not talking about being physically reborn, but he replied in the context of the Lord's analogy."[9]

Nicodemus appears to have been sincere in his query concerning the phrase *born again*. Unlike other Pharisees who constantly sought to trap Jesus, the text suggests that Nicodemus was simply being candid. Jesus replied, explaining exactly what he meant by this phrase, telling Nicodemus "…unless one is born of water and the Spirit he cannot enter into the kingdom of God" (v. 5).

The dual form of Jesus' answer (born of *water* and *the Spirit*) has led some to conclude that two distinct births are in view. The first term (born of water) is said to represent physical childbirth as a baby emerges from the womb. The rationale behind this view lies in the details of the human birthing process since, prior to birth, a child is enveloped by amniotic fluid in the mother's womb. The second term (born of the Spirit), it is argued, depicts the spiritual transformation one experiences during his/her conversion to Christianity.

Finding Bible commentaries that support this teaching can be a challenge since it is one of the less popular perspectives on this passage of Scripture. It is a viewpoint advanced mostly by laymen and, as a consequence, appears primarily in blogs and other less formal settings. Generally speaking, respected Bible scholars have dismissed it. Still, there are a few published writers, like Chuck Smith (1927-2013), who have espoused this view. According to Mr. Smith:

> Jesus said, 'That which is born of the flesh is flesh, but that which is born of the Spirit is spirit.' And so, He's talking about the two births: born of the water, and born of the Spirit. And that the born of the Spirit is referring to the new birth, the spiritual birth that we have, where born of the water would refer to the fleshly birth.[10]

---

[9] MacArthur, John, *The MacArthur New Testament Commentary*, https://www.gty.org/library/bibleqnas-library/QA0302/what-does-it-mean-to-be-born-of-water-and-spirit, Accessed February 19, 2018.

[10] Smith, Chuck, *Chuck Smith Bible Commentary*, https://www.studylight.org/commentaries/csc/john-3.html, accessed July 5, 2017.

Flesh is Flesh

Jesus followed verse five with a seemingly philosophical observation stating, "That which is born of the flesh is flesh, and that which is born of the Spirit is spirit" (v. 6). The combination of statements found in verses five and six provide what some see as a measure of support for the view that the phrase *born of water* represents childbirth. They believe that verse six is intended as a reflection of verse five with water corresponding to flesh and spirit corresponding to spirit.

What meaning lies behind the statement, "That which is born of the flesh is flesh, and that which is born of the Spirit is spirit" (v. 6)? The answer is a simple one. The words reflect the discussion to this point, but flesh does not point to water. It was Nicodemus who introduced physical birth into the conversation (v. 4). Jesus responded by introducing spiritual birth (v. 5), as opposed to physical birth, as an explanation for *born again*. He then contrasted the two births for Nicodemus's benefit (v. 6).

The birth of flesh introduced by Nicodemus is unrelated to the spiritual birth of which Jesus spoke. Jesus' statement, *born of water and the Spirit* (v. 5) serves not only as a re-statement of *born again* (v. 3), but also as a rebuttal of Nicodemus's awkward imagery of human rebirth (v. 4). In verse 6 Jesus distinguishes between the two births – physical birth, which Nicodemus had introduced through which men enter the physical world and spiritual birth (of water and the Spirit) through which they enter the kingdom of God.

Unless *One* is Born Again

Jesus told Nicodemus, "…unless one is born again" (v. 3) and then reiterated, "…unless one is born of water and the Spirit" (v. 5). Of note in these statements is the word "one." This word comes from the Greek *tis*, which can mean a *person* or an *object*. In this case, there can be no doubt that a *person* (human being) is in view. Other translations render it as "man" (21st Century KJV) and "someone" (CSB, HCSB). This meaning of *tis* adds an important element to Jesus' teaching. He was telling Nicodemus that a *person* must be born of water and the Spirit to enter God's kingdom.

A human being this side of the womb (tis) has already experienced physical childbirth. The suggestion that Jesus would tell Nicodemus, an adult, that he must first be born physically in order to be born spiritually is, on its face, nonsensical. It would be like Jesus telling Nicodemus, *first you must be human*. The hollowness of such an answer is self-evident. Notwithstanding his peculiar comment about re-entering his mother's womb (v. 4), Nicodemus seriously wondered about the meaning of the words *born again* (v. 3). Having heard the preaching of John the Baptist and Jesus, he must have suspected that these words held spiritual meaning, but he seemed to be unfamiliar with this phraseology.

Two Elements of One Birth

Most Bible scholars, regardless of their doctrinal views, recognize the futility of attempting to discount the parallel phrasing of Jesus' words. For one to be born again – cleansed and presented to God with the purity of a newborn babe – he must be born of water and the Spirit. To be born again is to be born of water and the Spirit. The second phrase is an explanation of the first and the first is enfolded within the second. The suggestion that the water of this verse might depict childbirth, distinct from spiritual birth, stretches biblical analysis beyond acceptable limits. While people differ on the meaning of the terminology, Bible scholars generally agree on this point. Here are some sample writings on the topic.

> ...we must take water and spirit together and relate this to one birth as in v. 3.[11]

> The new birth "of water and of the Spirit" is one birth, not two, despite there being two elements in it.[12]

> Though verse 4 does introduce the idea of physical birth into the context, the term for water is never used in this sense elsewhere in the New Testament.[13]

> As the condition of salvation, the two things are a concrete unit; the first not without the second, the second not without the first.[14]

> *Why did Jesus say to Nicodemus, "Except a man be born of water and the Spirit, he cannot enter the kingdom of God?"* To correct his mistake in supposing that Jesus spoke of a natural birth. The birth spoken of was to

---

[11] Wenham, G. J., Motyer, J. A., Carson, D. A., France, R. T., editors, *New Bible Commentary*, Inter-Varsity Press, Nottingham, England, 1994, p. 1031.
[12] Cottman, John, *Coffman's Commentaries on the Bible - John*, A.C.U Press, Abilene, TX, 1974, p. 87.
[13] Cottrell, Jack, *Baptism A Biblical Study*, College Press Publishing, Jopplin, MO, 1989., p. 31.
[14] Lange, Johanne, *Lange's Commentary on the Holy Scriptures: Critical, Doctrinal, and Homiletical*, https://www.studylight.org/commentaries/lcc/john-3.html, accessed July 22, 2017.

> follow begetting by the truth, and this is the reason why the Spirit is associated with the birth.[15]
>
> Water baptism and Spirit baptism have been said to be two halves of one act. That one act is entrance into the kingdom of God.[16]
>
> ...**water and the Spirit**: This is linked immediately with new birth. There is not much to commend the view that 'water' refers to physical birth, and 'the Spirit' to spiritual regeneration.[17]
>
> The fact that "born of water and the Spirit" further develops "born again" in 3: 3 suggests that one birth is in view rather than two.[18]

The notion that born of water might mean childbirth is an idea that grew out of the sixteenth century Reformation Movement as men began to challenge biblical teaching on the efficacy of baptism. In order to undo centuries of scholarship on baptism as a matter of salvation, those verses that associated baptism with redemption needed to be overcome.

In John 3: 5, Jesus revealed the redemptive significance of baptism, serving up a serious challenge for the Reformers. Consequently, it was necessary to replace the image of baptism with something more amenable to Reformed Theology. While some teach that born of water stands as a reference to physical childbirth, this view finds no support in the immediate or expanded context of the narrative, or in God's Word generally.

---

[15] Hurte, William, *The Restoration New Testament Commentary in Question and Answer Form: A Catechetical Commentary*, Old Paths Publishing Company, Rosemead, CA, 1964, p. 136

[16] McPherson, Joseph D., *BORN OF WATER, BORN OF THE SPIRIT - What Did Jesus Mean by Being "Born of Water?"*
http://www.fwponline.cc/v16n1/v16n1joemac.html, accessed July 23, 2017.

[17] Bruce, F. F., General Editor, *New International Bible Commentary*, Zondervan Publishing, Grand Rapids, MI, 1979, p. 1238.

[18] Kostenberger, Andreas, J., *Zondervan Illustrated Biblical Backgrounds Commentary*, Volume 2, Zondervan Publishing, Grand Rapids, MI 1984, p. 35.

Chapter 3
– Born of Water –
God's Word

Water and the Word

Some see Jesus' reference to water in John 3: 5 as an allusion to God's Word. The idea is that, in his exchange with Nicodemus, Jesus' words do not join baptism and the Spirit, but God's Word and the Spirit. It is not necessarily canonized Scripture that is in view, but certainly the gospel message by which men are saved. Constable states:

> Another popular view is that 'water' refers to the written Word of God and 'spirit' refers to the Holy Spirit. This figurative use of 'water' does exist in the New Testament. (cf. Ephesians 5: 26),[19]

In *The Wells of Living Water Commentary*, Robert E. Neighbour (1872-1945) penned the following comparable sentiment.

> In Ephesians we read 'that He might sanctify and cleanse it with the washing of water by the Word.' 1 Peter speaks thus: 'Being born again by the Word of God.' James said, 'Of His own will begat He us by the Word of Truth.'[20]

John Darby (1800-1882) was a nineteenth century Anglo-Irish priest and theologian whose writing has been described as *electric*. He is best-known for his development of the doctrine now known as pre tribulation

---

[19] Constable, Thomas, *Expository Notes of Dr. Thomas Constable*, https://www.studylight.org/commentaries/dcc/john-3.html, accessed June 25, 2017.
[20] Neighbour, Robert, *The Wells of Living Water Commentary*, https://www.studylight.org/commentaries/lwc/john-3.html, accessed July 3, 2017.

rapture (a doctrine he introduced in 1830). He also happened to espouse the view of the discussion in John 3: 5 that the water of which Jesus spoke serves as an allusion to God's Word.

> Nicodemus sees no farther than the flesh. The Lord explains Himself. Two things were necessary-to be born of water, and of the Spirit. Water cleanses. And, spiritually, in his affections, heart, conscience, thoughts, actions, etc., man lives, and in practice is morally purified, through the application, by the power of the Spirit, of the word of God, which judges all things, and works in us livingly new thoughts and affections. This is the water; it is withal the death of the flesh. The true water which cleanses in a Christian way came forth from the side of a dead Christ. He came by water and blood, in the power of cleansing and of expiation. He sanctifies the assembly by cleansing it through the washing of water by the word. Ye are clean through the word which I have spoken unto you. It is therefore the mighty word of God which, since man must be born again in the principle and source of his moral being, judges, as being death, all that is of the flesh.[21]

The Old Testament

In John 3, following a few words from Jesus as he spoke of water and the Spirit (v. 5), flesh and the Spirit (v. 6), and the comparative nature of spiritual birth and the mystery of the wind (v. 8), Nicodemus asked a question that Jesus deemed unworthy of one who claimed to be a student of God's Word. He queried, "How can these things be?" (v. 9). Jesus admonished the Pharisee, saying, "Are you the teacher of Israel and do not understand these things?" (v. 10).

The rebuke was likely aimed at the pseudo piety for which the Pharisees were known. If Nicodemus knew Scripture as well as he claimed, he should have understood these things. God's historical use of water for spiritual cleansing is undeniable. Water and blood are thematic in the Old Testament ceremonies as demonstrated consistently in the books of Leviticus and Numbers. Additionally, Beasley-Murray noted that "Rabbinic writings contain not a few references to the idea of a man becoming a 'new creature,' and the comparison of a proselyte to a new child is well known."[22]

Some believe Jesus' scolding of Nicodemus meant that the Pharisee should have seen a connection between rebirth and the Word. The Old

---

[21] Darby, John, *Darby's Synopsis of the New Testament*, https://www.studylight.org/commentaries/dsn/john-3.html, accessed July 14, 2017.
[22] Beasely-Murray, G. R., *Baptism in the New Testament*, William B. Eerdman's Publishing Company, Grand Rapids, MI, 1973, p. 227.

Testament does, indeed, intimate a connection between word and purity as is evident in these words from the Psalms.

> How can a young man keep his way pure?
> By keeping *it* according to Your word. (Psalm 119: 9)

With the following words, God was speaking to the nation of Israel through the prophet Ezekiel. Still, these words seem to suggest something beyond the physical nation of Israel with an eye, perhaps, on the spiritual descendants of Abraham, Isaac, and Jacob mentioned by Paul (Romans 9: 6).

> [25] Then I will sprinkle clean water on you, and you will be clean; I will cleanse you from all your filthiness and from all your idols. [26] Moreover, I will give you a new heart and put a new spirit within you; and I will remove the heart of stone from your flesh and give you a heart of flesh. [27] I will put My Spirit within you and cause you to walk in My statutes, and you will be careful to observe My ordinances. (Ezekiel 36: 25-27)

While the Psalms text identifies a link between purity and the word of God, it does not associate water with the word. Also, the rarity of verses like this in the Old Testament do not compare to the multitude of passages where water is depicted in connection with God's ordinances. In the book of Leviticus alone, water is depicted as a matter of purification more than 30 times and in the book of Numbers, at least a dozen times. Since Jesus expected Nicodemus to understand the meaning of his words, it seems he would have been far more likely to recognize the relationship between water and cleansing ordinances than purity and the word.

The New Testament

Robert Neighbour, cited earlier in this chapter, noted that Scripture associates the Word of God with spiritual rebirth more than once. Peter told his audience "…for you have been born again not of seed which is perishable but imperishable, *that is*, through the living and enduring word of God" (1 Peter 1: 23). Also, James told his readers "In the exercise of His will He brought us forth by the word of truth, so that we would be a kind of first fruits among His creatures" (James 1: 18). Additionally, Jesus told his disciples, "You are already clean because of the word which I have spoken to you" (John 15: 3).

The connection that these verses appear to offer between purity, spiritual rebirth (born again; brought us forth), and the word (word of God; word of truth, word which I have spoken) has led some to believe John 3 reflects these sentiments from Peter, James, and Jesus. It is said that born of water means born of the Word of God. The difficulty is that none of these verses connects *word* to *water*. Consequently, that association must be drawn elsewhere.

As Constable noted, some have advanced the view that Scripture bridges the gap between water and the word. Paul, in his letter to the Ephesians, likens Jesus and the church to a husband and his bride (Ephesians 5: 25). According to Paul, Christ loves the church in much the same way that a man loves his wife. Just as a man anticipates that his bride will be pure when she comes to him, so Jesus expects purity in the church.

No one comes to Christ as a pure, sinless individual. However, Christ, with fervent love, offers the cleansing by which his bride (the church) can be presented to him in a state of absolute purity. It is a purification that reflects the rebirth mentioned in John 3: 5. Paul told the Ephesians that the church is cleansed "…by the washing of water with the word" (Ephesians 5: 26). With this statement, it has been argued, Paul has provided what appears to be the necessary link between *water* and *the word* such that the water of John 3 might represent God's Word.

Coming into the presence of God (entering the kingdom/being presented as a bride) necessitates purity. This is the lesson behind both Jesus' instructions to Nicodemus and Paul's words to the Ephesians. It would be accurate to say that the primary biblical theme from Genesis through Revelation is God preparing humanity to enter his presence by purifying mankind from sin.

Many seem to leap to verses like John 15: 3, Ephesians 5: 26, 1 Peter 1: 23, and James 1: 18, to find a meaning for water in John 3: 5. They argue that Peter, James, and Jesus associate rebirth/purity with the word and Paul ties water to the word. Consequently, in John 3: 5, water could just as easily mean God's Word. It is said that the water of this verse is merely a figurative depiction illustrating that the Word has the same cleansing attributes spiritually as water might have against the flesh.

Logos vs. Rhema

It is one thing to speculate that *water* might represent the Word of God and to make that connection through Ephesians 5: 26; but it is another to explain *how* it represents God's Word in the context of Jesus' meeting with Nicodemus. After all, based on the words of Peter and James, does it not seem reasonable to presume that being *born of water* in John, where rebirth is in view, means born of the Word?

When *word* (Gr. *logos*) appears in Scripture, many people picture God's Word (the Bible). However, *logos* is used in various ways. At times it means simply to speak, or to make a statement, as in the following verses.

> Jesus said to him, 'Go; your son lives.' The man believed the word (logos) that Jesus spoke to him and started off. (John 4: 50)

> Now when the captain of the temple *guard* and the chief priests heard these words (logos), they were greatly perplexed about them as to what would come of this. (Acts 5: 24)

This use of *logos* is comparatively rare in Scripture. Other times, logos is used as a direct reference to Jesus. The Apostle John used this term to depict Jesus as an eternal member of the Godhead.

> [1] In the beginning was the Word (logos), and the Word (logos) was with God, and the Word (logos) was God…[14] And the Word (logos) became flesh, and dwelt among us, and we saw His glory, glory as of the only begotten from the Father, full of grace and truth. (John 1: 1, 14)

Generally, when *logos* appears in the New Testament, the best understanding, and arguably the best interpretation, is that it represents the English words *teaching(s)* or *instruction(s)* as in the following passages.

> Therefore everyone who hears these words (logos) of Mine and acts on them, may be compared to a wise man who built his house on the rock. (Matthew 7: 24)

> Truly, truly, I say to you, he who hears My word (logos), and believes Him who sent Me, has eternal life, and does not come into judgment, but has passed out of death into life. (John 5: 24)

Those who teach that born of water is intended to depict God's Word see it as either a spiritual birth in fulfillment of God's Word or a birth that is in accordance with God's teaching, or instruction. With both Peter and James declaring that people are born again with or through the word (logos), it does not seem unreasonable to conclude that in Jesus' words *born of water*, God's Word may be represented. It seems even more reasonable considering Paul's words to the Ephesians where he deliberately aligns cleansing with water and word (Ephesians 5: 26).

As enticing as this line of reasoning may be, there are certain things to consider before embracing it. The truth is, *logos* is not the only Greek word that is translated into English as *word*. Quite often the Greek word *rhema* is rendered *word* in English translations. This is a word that is suited to certain uses. It derives from *rheo* and takes on such meanings as *utterance* or *narration*. It is at times used in the context of verbal attacks (cf. Matthew 5: 11). Other times it is a matter of making a proclamation or declaration (cf. Luke 2: 17). This is relevant to this discussion in that it is *rhema*, not *logos*, that is translated *word* in the Ephesians passage.

The word *rhema* appears several dozen times in the New Testament in assorted settings and generally refers to the spoken word. In English versions of the Bible it is translated variously depending on the context. Here are several examples from the NIV.

> Simon answered, 'Master, we've worked hard all night and haven't caught anything. But because you say so (rhema), I will let down the nets.' (Luke 5: 5)

> He spoke these words (rhema) while teaching in the temple courts near the place where the offerings were put. Yet no one seized him, because his hour had not yet come. (John 8: 20)

> As Paul and Barnabas were leaving the synagogue, the people invited them to speak (rhema) further about these things on the next Sabbath. (Acts 13: 42)

> This will be my third visit to you. 'Every matter must be established by the testimony (rhema) of two or three witnesses.' (2 Corinthians 13: 1)

In the Bible, *rhema* is occasionally used, either figuratively or literally, to identify the word(s) of God. However, when that occurs, it is still used in reference to the *spoken* word or *proclamations*, as in these verses, also from the NIV.

> For the one whom God has sent speaks the words (rhema) of God, for God gives the Spirit without limit. (John 3: 34)

> But what does it say? 'The word (rhema) is near you; it is in your mouth and in your heart,' that is, the message (rhema) concerning faith that we proclaim: (Romans 10: 8)

Do you not believe that I am in the Father, and the Father is in Me? The words (rhema) that I say to you I do not speak on My own initiative, but the Father abiding in Me does His works. (John 14: 10))

By faith we understand that the universe was formed at God's command (rhema), so that what is seen was not made out of what was visible. (Hebrews 11: 3)

It is evident from these verses that *rhema* is not used in Scripture in the same sense as *logos*. What is the meaning of *rhema* in Ephesians? How is it used and how would it have been understood by the Christians in Ephesus? In what sense would Jesus have been *speaking* in connection with *washing of water*?

While English translations are by and large unified in translating *rhema* as *word* in Ephesians 5: 26, Greek interlinear Bibles and literal translations can offer some additional insight. Here is how this verse is rendered in *The Jerusalem Bible, The Simple English Bible*, and the direct translations found in *Young's Literal Translation* and *Scripture4All Interlinear Bible* respectively.

> …to make her holy. He made her clean by washing her in water **with a form of words**. – emphasis added

> He used a washing of water **through the message** to make God's people holy. – emphasis added

> …that he might sanctify it (the church), having cleansed [it] with the bathing of the water **in the saying** – emphasis added

> That her (the church) He should be hallowing to the bath of the water **in declaration** – emphasis added

These more literal translations paint a different picture from other English renderings. It is for this reason that Bible scholars have consistently recognized this washing as representative of the spiritual cleansing that occurs when one is immersed in the baptismal waters. Concerning this wording, the following authors all wrote prior to the twentieth century.

> *That he might sanctify and cleanse it* — Might remove the guilt, power, and pollution of sin; *with the washing of water* — in baptism.[23]

---

[23] Benson, Joseph, *Joseph Benson's Commentary of the Old and New Testaments*, https://www.studylight.org/commentaries/rbc/ephesians-5.html, accessed August 8, 2017.

Washing it with the washing of water. Having mentioned the inward and hidden sanctification, he now adds the outward symbol, by which it is visibly confirmed; as if he had said, that a pledge of that sanctification is held out to us by baptism...When Paul says that we are washed by baptism, his meaning is, that God employs it for declaring to us that we are washed, and at the same time performs what it represents.[24]

...with the washing of water — rather as *Greek,* 'with,' or 'by the *laver* of *the* water,' namely, *the* baptismal water. So it ought to be translated in Titus 3:5, the only other passage in the New Testament where it occurs.[25]

That he might sanctify and cleanse it . . .—The true rendering is, that He might sanctify it, having cleansed it in the laver of the water in [the] Word. The reference in 'the laver of the water' to baptism, is even more unquestionable than in 'the laver of regeneration' of Titus 3:5. Hence we must conclude that the phrase 'in the Word' is in some way connected with that sacrament. Of the two Greek words translated 'word,' the one here used is that which signifies not 'the word' existing as a definite thought in the mind, but 'the word' as audibly spoken.[26]

With the laver of the water, τῷ λούτρῳ τοῦ ὕδατος.—Unquestionably this means baptism; the readers must have thus understood it (Harless); *insigne testimonium de baptismo* (Bengel). The article (τῷ) denotes something well known; besides ὕδατος and the connection with καθαρίσας. Comp. Titus 3:5; 1 Corinthians 6:11; Hebrews 10:23; Acts 10:47; Acts 22:16. But the water does not give the cleansing which is spoken of, nor the bathing or washing. It is the baptism, not the bath in the water. Hence there is further added: **in the word**, ἐν ῥήματι, in order to designate Christian baptism as to its essence. The notion of baptism, as a means of cleansing beside the sanctifying (see Doctr. Notes 5, 6), as well as the position of this phrase require us to take both together, and the usage respecting the word ῥῆμα) and the connection by means of ἐν (like Ephesians 6:2 : ἐντολὴ ἐν ἐπαγγελίᾳ) admit of this.[27]

Calvin's identification of baptism as a sign/sacrament will be discussed a bit later, but it is significant that he recognized *water* as a clear reference to baptism in this text. Where Paul's words to the Ephesians are concerned, this picture of baptism has been

---

[24] Calvin, John, *Calvin's Commentary on the Bible*, https://www.studylight.org/commentaries/cal/ephesians-5.html, accessed August 18, 2017.
[25] Jamieson, Robert, A.R.Faucett, David Brown, *Commentary Critical and Explanatory of the Whole Bible*, http://classic.studylight.org/com/jfb/view.cgi?book=eph&chapter=005, accessed August 25, 2017.
[26] Ellicott, Charles, *Ellicott's Commentary for English Readers*, https://www.studylight.org/commentaries/ebc/ephesians-5.html, accessed August 25, 2017.
[27] Lange, Johanne, *Lange's Commentary on the Holy Scriptures: Critical, Doctrinal, and Homiletical* https://www.studylight.org/commentaries/lcc/ephesians-5.html, accessed August 21, 2017.

understood and accepted since the time of the apostles. Given the consistency of so many Bible scholars over nearly twenty centuries, it is difficult to escape the reality that modern attempts to dismiss baptism from Ephesians 5: 26 lie well outside the lines of principled scholarship.

What can be concluded from this with respect to the *washing with water* about which Paul wrote? The answer lies in the meaning of the words of this verse as rendered in the *Jerusalem Bible* and the literal translations cited above, and equally recognized in the accompanying commentaries. In this setting, *rhema* depicts either spoken words that are somehow connected to the washing that is taking place or to a statement/declaration that is made by, or is inherent in, the act itself.

There are three primary ways this verse can be read and understood. It could be that *rhema* points to the words that accompany baptism (i.e., in the name of the Father, Son, and Holy Spirit) as spoken by Jesus in what is known as the Great Commission (Matthew 28: 19). According to *The Expositor's Bible Commentary with the New International Version*:

> What is 'the word' that accompanies baptism? The Greek term *rhema* means something spoken – an utterance. It could refer to the preaching of the gospel at a baptismal service (1 Peter 1: 23-25) It is more likely, however, to indicate the formula used at the moment of baptism. In principle, this was Trinitarian in shape but on occasion it simply invoked the all-sufficient name of Jesus.[28]

The word could also represent one's confession of faith in Christ that undoubtedly accompanied baptism in the first century as it does today. This is the view espoused by *Commentary Critical and Explanatory on the Whole Bible*:

> by the word — *Greek,* 'IN the word.' To be joined with 'cleansing it,' or 'her.' The 'word of faith' (Romans 10:8, Romans 10:9, Romans 10:17), of which confession is made in baptism.[29]

These are reasonable views, but a candid reading of the text suggests that *rhema* might depict Jesus' declaration of purity that is recognized in *Scripture4All Interlinear Bible*. Paul seems to be saying that Jesus

---

[28] Boice, James, Wood, A. Skevington, *The Expositor's Bible Commentary with the New International Version: Galatians • Ephesians*, Zondervan Publishing House, Grand Rapids, MI, 1995, p. 179.

[29] Jamieson, Robert, A. R. Fausset, David Brown, *Commentary Critical and Explanatory on the Whole Bible*, https://www.studylight.org/commentaries/jfb/ephesians-5.html, accessed August 25, 2017.

provides both the cleansing and the declaration. Perhaps this declaration of purity is incorporated into the very act of *washing with water*, reflecting God's words of promise for the one who submits to the rite of baptism in Jesus' name. Calvin suggested this in his commentary and the same idea is expressed in the following words from G. R. Beasley-Murray:

> ...there is much to be said for declining to limit the reference in this context and to regard it as 'the word' in its broadest connotation – the Word of redemption and life that baptism itself enshrines...[30]

One blogger defends the claim that *born of water* in John 3: 5 represents God's Word. The following observation was made in an article titled, *What Does it Mean to be, "Born of Water?"*

> First, the words 'baptize' or 'baptism' occur approximately 85 times in Scripture. And even though this ritual is frequently mentioned, nowhere is it called, being 'born of water.' If someone wants to associate this term with baptism, the burden should be upon them to do so because Scripture doesn't make the connection.[31]

What has been left unsaid here is that John 3: 5 is the only verse in Scripture where the expression *born of water* appears. Consequently, neither is this phrase associated with God's Word elsewhere. Yet, the Apostle Paul connects rebirth/renewal directly to water baptism (Romans 6: 4) and an individual's entrance into the body of Christ (1 Corinthians 12: 13). It seems to be a considerable stretch to insist that the burden of proof should be placed upon those who recognize that connection.

In Scripture, being born again is associated with *logos* on occasion (James 1: 18; 1 Peter 1: 23). Yet, when the forgiveness and/or new life of a believer is associated with water (e.g., Mark 1: 4; Luke 3: 3; Romans 6: 1-4), baptism is unmistakably in view. Furthermore, water and baptism are tightly knit together in the New Testament (e.g., Matthew 3: 11; John 3: 23; Acts 1: 5; 8: 36; 10: 47; 1 Peter 3: 20-21). Additionally, there are passages, according to scholarly consensus, where the words water/washing/bath offer literary allusions to

---

[30] Beasely-Murray, G. R., *Baptism in the New Testament*, William B. Eerdman's Publishing Company, Grand Rapids, MI, 1973, pp 228-229.
[31] Bently, R. K., *John 3: 5 – What Does it Mean to be, "Born of Water?"* http://rkbentley.blogspot.com/2008/11/john-35-what-does-it-mean-to-be-born-of.html, accessed August 1, 2017.

Christian baptism (e.g., Corinthians 6: 11; Titus 3: 5; Hebrews 10: 22; 1 John 5: 6-8).

Jesus and John were not shy about using the word *logos*. This word appears 22 times in John's gospel. On 15 of those 22 occasions, it is the apostle reporting Jesus' words. If Jesus, like James and Peter, wanted to associate being born again with *logos* as he spoke with Nicodemus, he could have easily done that. However, he chose instead to explain that to be born again is to be born out of water and the Spirit.

In James, where rebirth is in view, *logos* represents the great truths that constitute God's Word. However, the *washing of water* of which Paul wrote in Ephesians 5: 26 is not tied to the Word (logos) of God, but to the spoken word (rhema) that is associated with a spiritual washing with water. It is reasonable to believe that *rhema* depicts Christ's declaration of a pure bride, which is the topic that is in view. Yet, this verse is the primary vehicle used to tie *water* to *logos* and inferentially supplant the water of John 3: 5 with the Word of God. In truth, to borrow the words from the blogger mentioned above, "Scripture doesn't make the connection."

The claim that water in John 3: 5 represents the Word of God is grounded strictly in English translations that render both *logos* and *rhema* as *word*. This doctrinal position finds no footing in the Greek text. When examining the logic used by many commentators who make the leap between *water* and *the word*, it becomes evident that most individuals who support this claim are unaware that two different Greek words are even in play in these passages. For those who are aware of the presence of the different words, it must either be dismissed as doctrinally irrelevant, presumed that the two words are fully interchangeable, or intentionally disregarded to satisfy doctrinal bias. The truth is, nothing about Jesus' exchange with Nicodemus suggests that he intended to use *water* to represent the Word of God.

Chapter 4
- Born of Water -
The Holy Spirit

The Water/Spirit Connection

The third position to be considered with respect to being born of water is held by some laymen as well as certain Bible scholars. The claim is that, in John 3: 5, water and spirit are simply two references to the Holy Spirit. This is an interesting approach to Jesus' words since the text appears to distinguish between water and spirit, suggesting that these are two distinct concepts even though they are closely bound in the verse. John Gill (1697-1771), a post-Reformation English Baptist pastor was an early proponent of this view, stating:

> …except a man be born of water and of the Spirit: these are, 'two words', which express the same thing…the grace of the Spirit of God.[32]

The premise upon which this view is built focuses on the Greek conjunction *kai*, which is translated into English as "and." In Jesus' words to Nicodemus, the word *kai* appears as a connector between water and (kai) the Spirit. The argument is made that *kai* might be translated into English as the adverb *even*. Using what is said to be an interpretive solution to the text, the claim is that the verse could be read "born of water, *which is* the Spirit." With this idea in view, consider the following comments from *Believer's Bible Commentary*:

---

[32] Gill, John, *Gill's Exposition of the Entire Bible*, http://biblehub.com/john/3-5.htm, accessed August 22, 2017.

...the word translated 'and' could just as correctly have been translated "even." Thus, the verse would read: **Unless one is born of water,** *even* **the Spirit, he cannot enter the kingdom of God.** We believe that this is the correct meaning of the verse.[33]

There is at least one occasion within the pages of God's Word where water is understood to speak figuratively of the Holy Spirit. It occurs later in the gospel of John and, like John 3: 5, involves words spoken by Jesus. At the Festival of Tabernacles in Judea Jesus clashed with the Jews who were in attendance, but he turned those conflicts into teaching opportunities. On the last day of the festival he made a public address, sharing the following thoughts.

> [37] Now on the last day, the great *day* of the feast, Jesus stood and cried out, saying, "If anyone is thirsty, let him come to Me and drink. [38] He who believes in Me, as the Scripture said, 'From his innermost being will flow rivers of living water.'" [39] But this He spoke of the Spirit, whom those who believed in Him were to receive; for the Spirit was not yet *given*, because Jesus was not yet glorified. (John 7: 37-39)

Since Jesus used the term *living water* to picture the Holy Spirit, it seems reasonable to infer that other times when he used similar language, it was intended to represent the Holy Spirit. For instance, this was undoubtedly what Jesus had in mind as he offered the Samaritan woman *living water* that would quench a spiritual thirst (John 4: 10). It also stands to reason that this same meaning could apply to the mysterious *water of life* mentioned in John's apocalyptic vision (Revelation 7: 17; 21: 6; 22: 1, 17). Could that same meaning apply in Jesus' discussion with Nicodemus? Renowned scholar Clinton Lockhart, in his work titled *Principles of Interpretation*, made an important observation that is germane to this line of reasoning, commenting:

> The literal or most usual meaning of a word, if consistent, should be preferred to a figurative or less usual signification.[34]

Jesus used the expression *living water* as a reference to the Holy Spirit. The same can be inferred in other passages where comparable

---

[33] MacDonald, William, *Believer's Bible Commentary*, Thomas Nelson Publishers, Nashville, Atlanta, London, Vancouver, 1995, p. 1478.
[34] Lockhart, Clinton. *Principles of Interpretation Revised Edition*, Gospel Light Publishing Company, Delight, AR, p. 160.

language appears. However, interpretive principles are strained when it is insisted that a "less usual signification," which appears rarely in Scripture, must apply in a setting where the language does not require it and the literal meaning of the word can be suitably assigned.

While many, beginning with the Reformation Movement, began to question the efficacy of baptism with respect to salvation, no one doubted the nature of Christian baptism. It is the repentant person's submission to immersion in water that is in view in Scripture. Certainly, there are occasions in God's Word where a form of the term *baptism* is used figuratively and does not refer to John's baptism, the baptism performed by Jesus' disciples, or Christian immersion in water (e.g., Mark 10: 38-39; Acts 1: 5; 1 Corinthians 10: 2), but these are rare.

An Anglican clergyman by the name of E. W. Bullinger (1837-1913) was among the first to be so bold as to challenge that view. He taught that when the word *baptism* appears in the New Testament, it is not necessarily water baptism that is in view. Instead, it serves as a reference to Christ immersing individuals in the Spirit per the prophecy of John the Baptist (John 1: 33). He saw this as a baptism that excluded water. This principle he then applied to several passages where the terms baptism or water appear and the rite of baptism (immersion in water) had been perceived for nearly two millennia (c.f. Romans 6: 3-4; 1 Corinthians 12: 13; Ephesians 5: 26; Titus 3: 5).

Bullinger took this same approach where John 3: 5 is concerned, insisting that the term *water* is not to be understood as physical water, but is being employed figuratively to speak of the Holy Spirit or, as Bullinger put it, *spiritual water*. He wrote:

> ...of water and spirit...Not two things, but one, by which the latter Noun becomes a superlative and emphatic Adjective, determining the meaning and nature of the former Noun, showing that one to be spiritual water: i.e. not water but spirit. It is to be rendered 'of water-yea, spiritual water'.[35]

Even

English Bible translations generally render *kai* as *and* in John 3: 5.[36] Translating *kai* as *even* requires not only a historic shift in understanding the Greek text, but it involves recharacterizing *kai*, which is a coordinating conjunction, into *even*, which is an adverb.

---

[35] Bullinger, E. W., *E. W. Bullinger's Companion Bible Notes*, https://www.studylight.org/commentaries/bul/john-3.html, Accessed August 15, 2017.
[36] The AMPC adds *even* parenthetically following *and*. Also, the CEV reads "born not only by water, but by the Spirit." The implication in the CEV is "but (also) by the Spirit."

The word *even* appears countless times in every English Bible translation and it is important to appreciate the Greek from which the term is derived as well as its use in each verse where it appears. If it is true that "...the word translated 'and' could just as correctly have been translated 'even,'"[37] Scripture should bear this out. If, however, God's Word does not support that premise, the belief that *water* might mean *the* S*pirit* in John 3: 5 must be dismissed.

For simplicity's sake, the focus here will be on the four gospels and the NASB. Below is a passage from each gospel letter where *even* is not translated from the Greek *kai*. Consider these sample verses.

> And whoever in the name of a disciple gives to one of these little ones **even** a cup of cold water to drink, truly I say to you, he shall not lose his reward. (Matthew 10: 42) – emphasis added

> And He came home, and the crowd gathered again, to such an extent that they could not **even** eat a meal. (Mark 3: 20) – emphasis added

> And behold, **even** your relative Elizabeth has also conceived a son in her old age; and she who was called barren is now in her sixth month. (Luke 1: 36) – emphasis added

> For not **even** the Father judges anyone, but He has given all judgment to the Son, (John 5: 22) – emphasis added

This use of the English word *even* is found numerous times in Scripture. However, it is the manner of use that is important. In each case, it constitutes what is known in English as a scalar particle and is used in an adverbial sense. According to the website languagelog.ldc, this use of the word began to develop somewhere around the sixteenth century (coincidently with the advent of the Reformation Movement). In an article on that site entitled *What does "even" even mean?*, the following observation has been made:

> According to the OED,[38] *even* started out meaning 'flat, level, uniform', passed through related notions like 'equal, coincident, balanced, exact', and eventually came to be used 'in weakened senses as an intensive or emphatic

---

[37] MacDonald, William, *Believer's Bible Commentary*, Thomas Nelson Publishers, Nashville, Atlanta, London, Vancouver, 1995, p. 1478.
[38] OED stands for Oxford English Dictionary.

particle', which might be 'Prefixed to a subject, object, or predicate, or to the expression of a qualifying circumstance, to emphasize its identity'.[39]

Emphasis of identity is precisely how the word is applied in the above-mentioned verses. The purpose of *even* is to communicate a sense of significance. However, what is most interesting is that, in these verses, the word is not found in the Greek manuscripts. Not one of the verses cited above contains a Greek word that can be translated into English as *even*. The word was incorporated into English versions by the translators because they believed it helped accentuate in English the force that the Greek intended to convey.

There are times, however, when the English word *even* is translated from a word found in the Greek text. Remaining with the gospels and the NASB, below is one example from each of the gospels to demonstrate how the word is used as well as the Greek from which it is drawn.

> [9] Do not acquire gold, or silver, or copper for your money belts, [10] or a bag for *your* journey, or **even** two coats, or sandals, or a staff; for the worker is worthy of his support. (Matthew 10: 9-10) – emphasis added

> Not **even** in this respect was their testimony consistent. (Mark 14: 59) – emphasis added

> But the news about Him was spreading **even** farther, and large crowds were gathering to hear *Him* and to be healed of their sicknesses. (Luke 5: 15) – emphasis added

> As Moses lifted up the serpent in the wilderness, **even** so must the Son of Man be lifted up. (John 3: 14) – emphasis added

The word *even* is used in various ways in these verses. For instance, in the verse from Matthew, *even* is translated from the Greek conjunction *mede* meaning *nor* or, as it is translated in the KJV, *nor yet*. Mark uses the Greek *oude houtos*, which literally reads something like *not yet thus*, where *oude* is *not yet* and *houtos* carries the adverbial meaning of *thus* (as a result). Consequently, this phrase is translated into English in the NASB as *not even*. In Luke, the word *even* is drawn from the Greek *mallon*, again in an adverbial sense, meaning *still more* or *so much the more*, Thus, the NASB reads *even farther*. In this case, *even*

---

[39] Liberman, Mark, *What does "even" even mean?* http://languagelog.ldc.upenn.edu/nll/?p=2943, accessed August 12, 2017.

does not stand alone, but is incorporated into the idea of advancement that is at the heart of the word *mallon*. Like Mark 14: 59, John uses the Greek *houtos* as an adverb meaning *thus* or *consequently* (as a result). However, without its negative counterpart *oude*, meaning *not yet*, this time *houtos* stands alone resulting in the translation *even so*.

While this is a lot of information to take in, the hope is that it can be simplified. To that end, following are these same four verses as they appear in *Young's Literal Translation*. The point of this translation is to give an English rendering of Scripture that reflects as closely as possible a direct translation based purely on the wording of the original languages.

> [9] 'Provide not gold, nor silver, nor brass in your girdles, [10] nor scrip for the way, **nor** two coats, nor sandals, nor staff -- for the workman is worthy of his nourishment. (Matthew 10: 9-10) – emphasis added

> And **neither** so was their testimony alike. (Mark 14: 59) – emphasis added

> ...but **the more** was the report going abroad concerning him, and great multitudes were coming together to hear, and to be healed by him of their infirmities, (Luke 5: 15) – emphasis added

> And as Moses did lift up the serpent in the wilderness, **so** it behoveth the Son of Man to be lifted up, (John 3: 14) – emphasis added

Kai

It is also true that the Greek *kai* is, on occasion, rendered *even* in some English Bible translations. Following are a few examples from the NASB of how the term is used. For the sake of consistency and simplicity, these verses also come from the four gospel letters.

> For if you love those who love you, what reward do you have? Do not even (kai) the tax collectors do the same? (Matthew 5: 46)

> For whoever has, to him *more* shall be given; and whoever does not have, even (kai) what he has shall be taken away from him. (Mark 4: 25)

> If you love those who love you, what credit is *that* to you? For even (kai) sinners love those who love them. (Luke 6: 32)

> [16] But even if I do judge, My judgment is true; for I am not alone *in it*, but I and the Father who sent Me. [17] Even (kai) in your law it has been written that the testimony of two men is true. (John 8: 16-17)

In each of these verses where *kai* is translated *even*, the word is again employed as a conjunction. Specifically, it is used here to connect two statements or ideas. In these cases, the word *even* is best understood to mean *also*. Below are these same verses cited from *Young's Literal Translation*.

> For, if ye may love those loving you, what reward have ye? do not also (kai) the tax-gatherers the same? (Matthew 5: 46)

> ...for whoever may have, there shall be given to him, and whoever hath not, also (kai) that which he hath shall be taken from him. (Mark 4: 25)

> ...if ye love those loving you, what grace have ye? for also (kai) the sinful love those loving them; (Luke 6: 32)

> [16] and even if I do judge my judgment is true, because I am not alone, but I and the Father who sent me; [17] and also (kai) in your law it hath been written, that the testimony of two men are true. (John 8: 16-17)

When *kai* is translated into English with the word *even,* it does not change the character of *kai*. In each of these verses, it serves as a conjunction to connect two statements. YLT employs the translation *also* in these verses. While it is true that the word *also* is an adverb, it is what is known as a *conjunctive adverb*. According to the website natureofwriting.com, "A conjunctive adverb is an adverb that functions like a conjunction. Simply put, it ties together two independent clauses or sentences."[40] Therefore, its use here is appropriate. This represents the common use of *kai* in Scripture and in the Greek language generally.

The King James Bible

Many Bible scholars continue to insist that *kai* could be used as an adverb and rendered *even* in John 3: 5, concluding that water and the Spirit, in this context, are one and the same. Those who teach this believe that *kai* is intended to emphasize the spiritual, as opposed to physical, nature of the water mentioned in the verse. Does this use of *kai* appear in God's Word? To further investigate this possibility, four verses, one from each gospel, are offered here where this specific language appears. The idea is that something, or someone, is initially mentioned in the text and then an alternate identity or characteristic is

---

[40] https://natureofwriting.com/conjunctive-adverbs/, accessed December 27, 2018

offered with emphasis provided by the English word *even*. These verses are cited using the KJV.

> But be not ye called Rabbi: for one is your Master, **even** Christ; and all ye are brethren. (Matthew 23: 8) – emphasis added

> For all they did cast in of their abundance; but she of her want did cast in all that she had, **even** all her living. (Mark 12: 44) – emphasis added

> And when he was come nigh, **even** now at the descent of the mount of Olives, the whole multitude of the disciples began to rejoice and praise God with a loud voice for all the mighty works that they had seen; (Luke 19: 37) – emphasis added

> Ye do the deeds of your father. Then said they to him, We be not born of fornication; we have one Father, **even** God. (John 8: 41) – emphasis added

While these verses use *even* to emphasize oneness, there is weakness in applying this strategy to John 3: 5. Recognizing the equivalence of "Master…Christ" in Matthew, "all that she had…all her living" in Mark, "when he was come…now" in Luke, and "Father…God" in John, there is something very revealing in the Greek text. The word *kai* is not found in any of these verses. Thus, the word *even* is not translated from *kai*.

This use of the English word *even* in these settings represents a literary device found primarily in the KJV and its derivatives (21st Century King James Version, Authorized King James Version, New King James Version). It appears in certain other translations to a lesser degree (e.g., ASV, 1599 Geneva Bible), but is employed several dozen times in the KJV. However, it is not derived from the original language. Appendix A lists nearly fifty verses from the KJV where this construction is used. Not one of those verses involves the word *kai*.

The fact that the writers of the KJV had an affinity for the word *even* is found in their comparative use of the word. For instance, the word *even* appears several hundred more times in the KJV than the NIV. The same is true when comparing the KJV to the ESV, HCSB, NASB, NKJV, NRSV, RSV, etc. English versions that rival the KJV where their use of *even* is concerned include the ASV and 1599 Geneva Bible where it is used similarly.

When *kai* is translated into English with the word *even*, it is generally understood to mean *also*, or *in addition to*. It is conjunctive in nature, showing the connection between two or more subjects. Those who insist that *kai* could be translated *even* in John 3: 5 are offering a translation that finds no support in the Greek wording of the text.

When someone attempts to make the case that Jesus' words to Nicodemus might read *born of water, even the Spirit*, that argument is always prefaced with the claim that *kai* is often translated into English using the word *even*. Yet, it is not the case that kai is *often* so translated, much less as an adverb. Also, on its face this reveals that the assertion is not drawn from the original language but is grounded purely in English translations – specifically the 1599 Geneva Bible and the KJV, which was published in 1611.

This literary mechanism was first introduced onto the biblical landscape in the late sixteenth and early seventeenth centuries. Given that fact, it is not possible to successfully argue that this is what Jesus had in mind in the first century. This interpretation could not have been offered at the time because Scripture was not available in English.

Exceptions to the Rule

It is important to always treat Scripture with the respect it deserves. The truth is, the KJV does, on rare occasion, employ the English word *even* as a translation for *kai* in the manner that has been suggested for John 3: 5. It is important to address these exceptions to the norm. Below are five verses where this occurs.

> That ye may with one mind and one mouth glorify God, even (kai) the Father of our Lord Jesus Christ. (Romans 15: 6)

> Then cometh the end, when he shall have delivered up the kingdom to God, even (kai) the Father; when he shall have put down all rule and all authority and power. (1 Corinthians 15: 24)

> Blessed be God, even (kai) the Father of our Lord Jesus Christ, the Father of mercies, and the God of all comfort. (2 Corinthians 1: 3)

> To the end he may establish your hearts unblameable in holiness before God, even (kai) our Father, at the coming of our Lord Jesus Christ with all his saints. (1 Thessalonians 3: 13)

> Therewith bless we God, even (kai) the Father; and therewith curse we men, which are made after the similitude of God. (James 3: 9)

In these verses, the Greek wording literally translates as "the God and (kai) Father." This is the proper rendering of these verses and it is found in nearly all English Bible translations. The KJV translators chose to shift the position of the Greek word *to* (the) in order to connect it with *Father* rather than *God* as it appears in the Greek. Their fondness for the word *even* as a tool of emphasis evidently drove this decision.

While many proponents of the KJV openly criticize and even denounce the NKJV, it is interesting to note that the restructuring of these verses that took place in the KJV was corrected in the NKJV. In the NKJV, these verses are written "the God and Father." Those involved evidently recognized that the original KJV did not say in English what was written in Greek.

It is also true that God and Father are inherently one. By their very nature they are one. The Greek language need not be unduly manipulated to make that case. For this reason, the restructuring of the language by the KJV translators had no effect on the meaning of these verses.

There are a couple of instances in the New Testament where an unusual literary device involves the word *kai*. In Romans, as *kai* is translated into English with the word *even*, the item following *kai* represents a subset of that which precedes it.

> [23] And that he might make known the riches of his glory on the vessels of mercy, which he had afore prepared unto glory, [24] Even (kai) us, whom he hath called, not of the Jews only, but also of the Gentiles? (Romans 9: 23-24, KJV)

The term *vessels of mercy* (v. 23) identifies all those who are saved. Paul then recognizes himself and his companions as being *among* the saved (v. 24). The following shows how this passage is written in the Amplified Bible and the NRSV respectively.

> [23] And what if He has done so to make known the riches of His glory to the objects of His mercy, which He has prepared beforehand for glory, [24] *including* (kai) us, whom He also called, not only from among the Jews, but also from among the Gentiles? (Romans 9: 23-24)

> [23] and what if he has done so in order to make known the riches of his glory for the objects of mercy, which he has prepared beforehand for glory— [24] including (kai) us whom he has called, not from the Jews only but also from the Gentiles? (Romans 9: 23-24)

The essence of the message is, *vessels of mercy...including us* (and us). In this case, *vessels of mercy* does not equal *us*. The two are distinct

43

but related. In this instance, *kai* is used to make that connection. Paul offers an example of a similar use of *kai* when writing to the church in Thessalonica when explaining how much he and his companions would like to visit them. Here is that verse.

> Wherefore we would have come unto you, even (kai) I Paul, once and again; but Satan hindered us. (1 Thessalonians 2: 18, KJV)

Paul presents himself as a subset of *we*, emphasizing the fact that he personally, out of those mentioned in the text, had hoped to visit the Thessalonians. This represents the same unusual use of *kai*, but a couple of English versions seem to have found the appropriate words to express it. They include *The Living Bible* and *The New Living Translation* respectively. Again, the coordinating conjunction *and* is presented as the most reasonable rendering of *kai* in this verse.

> We wanted very much to come to you, and (kai) I, Paul, tried again and again, but Satan prevented us. (1 Thessalonians 2: 18)

> We wanted very much to come, and (kai) I, Paul, tried again and again, but Satan stopped us. (1 Thessalonians 2: 18)

In the first five verses listed in this section, notwithstanding the KJV rendering, *kai* is treated as a conjunction. The English word *and* represents a proper translation in those instances. In the KJV, the original Greek had to be circumvented in order to fit *even* into the English translation.

The final two texts are anomalies. Each one represents an unusual use of *kai*, presenting Paul (and his companions) as a subset of a larger group while, at the same time, distinguishing them from the rest of the group. In these verses the English conjunction *and* is the best interpretation of *kai*. Neither of these verses employs the term in a way that aligns with the meeting between Jesus and Nicodemus so that water could be regarded as a reference to the Spirit.

What men have failed to recognize is that if this construction could have been applied in John 3: 5 and *kai* could have been fittingly translated as *even* in this context to identify water as the Spirit, the translators of the KJV undoubtedly would have gone there. They were not shy about their use of this technique and this verse would have provided a perfect opportunity to continue that pattern. Yet, where Jesus' discourse with the Pharisee is concerned, like all other English versions of Scripture, they translated *kai* with the conjunction *and*, stipulating a connection, as well as a certain degree of separation, between water and the Spirit.

Verb-Preposition-Noun-Kai-Noun

Did Jesus intend to portray water and the Spirit in a singular sense? In other words, does water mean Spirit in John 3: 5 or are these, as the wording suggests, two distinct but related elements of rebirth? Perhaps the best way to gain a proper understanding of what Jesus intended with these words is to find comparable language in Scripture.

Jesus' statement concerning water and the Spirit involves the sequence of a verb followed by a prepositional phrase. However, it is not merely a prepositional phrase. In this case the preposition *of* has two objects attached to it. The first is *water* and the second is *the Spirit*. These objects are separated by the Greek *kai*, which is translated *and*. This kind of syntax appears multiple times in Scripture. The issue that must be addressed is how water and the Spirit are related in this verse. Does Jesus use the term *water* to represent *the Spirit*, or is something else in view?

A comparable use of this syntax appears in Luke's gospel where he wrote about Joseph and Mary's trek from Galilee to Bethlehem just prior to Jesus' birth. Luke wrote:

> Joseph also went up from Galilee, from the city of Nazareth, to Judea, to the city of David which is called Bethlehem, because he **was** (verb) **of** (preposition) **the house** (noun) **and** (kai) **family** (noun) of David. (Luke 2: 4) – emphasis added

What is interesting about this verse is that *house* and *family*, which are the two objects of the same preposition, are indeed synonymous. Each is connected to the preposition *of*, but they are also both connected with the prepositional phrase *of David*. That is to say Joseph was *of the house of David* and *of the family of David*. In this case, the *house of David* is the *family of David*. Both point to Joseph's familial relationship with David. Thomas Coke (1747-1814) wrote concerning this passage:

> Joseph is said to be of the house and *lineage of David,* which Dr. Doddridge renders, of *the family and household of David;* supposing with Grotius, that it refers to the divisions of the tribes into *families* and *households*. Compare Numbers 1:18; Numbers 1:54. In this sense of the words, after having told us that Joseph was of the *house of David,* it would have been very unnecessary

to add, he was also of his *family;* but it was not improper to say, that he was of his *family* and *household*.[41]

While Coke distinguishes between *family* and *household*, these terms are generally considered synonymous in Scripture. That is the case made by those who insist that, in John 3: 5, water and the Spirit are synonymous. This verse, it is argued, supports the claim that these two objects are one and the same, and that *water* is simply another way of saying *the Spirit*. However, there are issues that make it difficult to use this verse as a basis of support for that argument.

The first matter that makes the comparison problematic is that, like God and Father in the previous section, the house and family of David are naturally synonymous. The house of David is, by definition, the family of David. The Greek *kai* need not be translated into English in an exceptional and illusory manner to make it so. However, if, as Coke suggests, *kai* is meant to distinguish between family and household, this, too, would fail to support the view that water and the Spirit are one in John 3: 5. Another excellent example of this is found in the following verse late in the gospel of John.

> Jesus said to her, "Stop clinging to Me, for I have not yet ascended to the Father; but go to My brethren and say to them, 'I **ascend** (verb) to (preposition) **My Father** (noun) **and** (kai) **your Father** (noun), **and** (kai) **My God** (noun) **and** (kai) **your God** (noun).'" (John 20: 17) – emphasis added

In this example, the terms *My Father* and *your Father* are naturally one and the same as are the phrases *My God* and *your God*. No special translation of *kai,* and no unlikely interpretation of the verse, is necessary for the reader to recognize the oneness of these expressions. They point to the same being.

On the other hand, water and the Spirit are not naturally exchangeable. Water is distinct from the Spirit and they are addressed individually throughout Scripture. It is true that in Holy Writ water is occasionally presented in a manner that figuratively represents the Spirit, but that use is rare and is generally made evident in the narrative (e.g., *living water* or *water of life*).

Where the verb-preposition-noun-kai-noun formula is found in Scripture, the two objects of the preposition are commonly two distinct

---

[41] Coke, Thomas, *Thomas Coke Commentary on the Holy Bible*, https://www.studylight.org/commentaries/tcc/luke-2.html, accessed April 26, 2018.

elements. This seems to be the case when the nouns are not innately synonymous (viz., house/family). Following are some examples:

> As for me, I baptize you with water for repentance, but He who is coming after me is mightier than I, and I am not fit to remove His sandals; He will **baptize** (verb) you **with** (preposition) **the Holy Spirit** (noun) **and** (kai) **fire** (noun). (Matthew 3: 11) – emphasis added

> But an hour is coming, and now is, when the true worshipers will **worship** (verb) the Father **in** (preposition) **spirit** (noun) **and** (kai) **truth** (noun); for such people the Father seeks to be His worshipers. (John 4: 23) – emphasis added

> This is the One who **came** (verb) **by** (preposition) **water** (noun) **and** (kai) **blood** (noun), Jesus Christ; not with the water only, but with the water and with the blood. (1 John 5: 6) – emphasis added

These verses represent the common biblical use of this phrasing and it is common biblical use that must guide interpretation in John 3: 5. Unlike Luke 2: 4 and John 20: 17, the objects in the prepositional phrases are not inherently interchangeable. The *Holy Spirit* cannot be made to mean *fire* in Matthew. Scholars often disagree on what is meant by *fire* in this instance – whether it is intended to indicate purification or punishment – but it is generally understood that, in this verse, *fire* is not simply another way of saying *the Holy Spirit*. They are not the same. Cottrell wrote concerning this distinction:

> The strongest argument for this view is the grammatical construction of the phrase 'in the Holy Spirit and fire.' Here there is only one preposition (Greek, "en"; English, "in") governing the two objects, 'thus most naturally indicating one baptism composed of two elements' (Larry Chouinard, College Press NIV commentary on Matthew, p. 71).[42]

No doubt it would be impossible to worship God in *spirit* (or spiritually) without worshiping him in *truth*, but *truth* and *spirit* are distinct complementary elements of worship. Additionally, John identifies Jesus as "...One who came by water and blood." Yet, water and blood are easily and necessarily distinguished from one another in the text. They are complementary, but not the same. That distinction is

---

[42] Cottrell, Jack, *What Is the Meaning of the "Baptism in Fire" in Matthew 3:11?* http://jackcottrell.com/notes/what-is-the-meaning-of-the-baptism-in-fire-in-matthew-311/, accessed April 27, 2018.

made clear later in the verse as he wrote "...not with the **water** only, but with the **water** and with the **blood**" – emphasis added.

The terms *water* and *the Spirit* are not naturally interchangeable. That is to say, water is not, by definition, the Spirit, nor is the Spirit, by definition, water. Just as spirit and truth are complementary components of worship (John 4: 23), so water and the Spirit in John 3: 5 are distinct, complementary elements of the rebirth of which Jesus spoke. This represents the common biblical use as well as the common Greek use of this syntax and it is a truth that is plainly evident in a candid reading of the text. Thus, it is the only reasonable application of *kai* in John 3: 5.

Honest biblical analysis soundly refutes the claim that *kai* is commonly used as an adverb and should be applied thusly in John 3: 5. On those rare occasions when *kai* has been translated into English as *even*, it still serves as a coordinating conjunction. At no time does God's Word, in either the original language or English translations, provide support for the position that, "the word translated 'and' could just as correctly have been translated 'even.'"[43] For this reason no English version of the Bible offers that translation.

---

[43] MacDonald, William, *Believer's Bible Commentary*, Thomas Nelson Publishers, Nashville, Atlanta, London, Vancouver, 1995, p. 1478.

Chapter 5

– Born of Water –
John's Baptism

The Design of John's Gospel

It can be difficult at times to determine the exact purpose of certain narratives in Scripture. Much of the time inference must be made about the purpose based on what can be drawn from a passage or how the lessons provided affect those involved. Fortunately, where the gospel of John is concerned, the author's purpose is spelled out in no uncertain terms.

> [30] Therefore many other signs Jesus also performed in the presence of the disciples, which are not written in this book; [31] but these have been written so that you may believe that Jesus is the Christ, the Son of God; and that believing you may have life in His name. (John 20: 30-31)

John wrote his gospel so that men may know Jesus as the Messiah and as a result gain an eternal reward. Everything in this gospel is written with this goal in mind. The evidence John presented to make his case is found in his recording of the many miracles Jesus performed (including the narrative surrounding those miracles) and the wisdom of the teaching he offered.

Jesus' exchange with Nicodemus falls under the category *the wisdom of the teaching he offered*. Jesus' words on that occasion were aimed at teaching Nicodemus about obtaining an eternal reward since, with the words *born of water and the Spirit*, Jesus offered Nicodemus instruction on entering the kingdom of God.

John's gospel can be easily partitioned since it has some distinct shifts in focus. The first section is found in the first three chapters where Jesus and John the Baptist are introduced. The next section, where John features Jesus' interaction with people and the miracles he performed, involves chapters four through eleven. Beginning with the twelfth chapter, the apostle highlights the final week of Jesus' life from his visit to the house of Lazarus, whom he had recently raised from the dead (John 11: 1-44), through his post-resurrection interaction with the disciples. The focus here will be on the first section since it includes Jesus' encounter with Nicodemus.

The letter begins with the author, the Apostle John, introducing two individuals. He introduces Jesus as the Son of God calling him the Word (logos) in the first chapter (vv. 1-5). He follows this with an introduction of John the Baptist who served as the forerunner of the Messiah, also in the first chapter (vv. 6-28). With John's emphasis on *baptism of repentance for the forgiveness of sins*, it is not surprising that the apostle mentions baptism several times. In fact, in the first three chapters of this gospel, baptism is mentioned a total of ten times.

Water is mentioned eight times in this first section. Three times it refers to the wedding party where Jesus turned water into wine. On four occasions (not counting John 3: 5), it is discussed in connection with baptism. When a single topic is discussed consistently over a stretch of three chapters, it is safe to say that this is a primary focus of those chapters if not *the* primary focus. In this case it is at the very heart of the narrative.

Jesus' exchange with Nicodemus falls within a segment of Scripture where the topic of baptism is at the forefront. Not only is baptism the dominant subject under consideration, but it is defined repeatedly in terms of water (John 1: 26, 31, 33; 3: 23). Additionally, water is mentioned in the second chapter as Jesus turned water into wine (John 2: 1-10). It can be stated positively, then, that the water mentioned in these chapters consistently refers to the physical substance of water. John baptized in the Jordan River (John 1: 28) and Jesus turned water into wine.

Scripture was not thrown together haphazardly and the precise location of Jesus' talk with Nicodemus in John's gospel is no coincidence. It is positioned here for a reason. In the midst of a section of Scripture focused on water and baptism, Jesus told Nicodemus, "...unless one is born of water and the Spirit he cannot enter into the kingdom of God" (John 3: 5).

Many people insist that Jesus' reference to water must mean something (anything) other than immersion in water. For centuries men have jumped through extraordinary analytical hoops to convince that the water of this verse is a figure of something else. It is said that the surrounding narrative, where John's baptism is in view and where water means water, is not germane to the conversation between Jesus and Nicodemus and is, therefore, immaterial. Why would anyone be so willing to ignore the context of a passage of Scripture? It is because their explanation of the text collapses under its weight.

It defies hermeneutic principles to insist that the surrounding narrative must be set aside in determining the meaning of Jesus' words. Context is not only always relevant, but it is always important. Honest biblical analysis can only lead to the conclusion that Jesus was teaching Nicodemus a tenet that is supported time and again in God's Word. Baptism – immersion in water – is the God-appointed moment of redemption, the forgiveness of sins. This ties in nicely with John's baptism of repentance, which is the primary topic in this section of Scripture.

The Nature of John the Baptist's Ministry

John the Baptist's ministry was intended to help mankind, and particularly the Jewish nation, transition to God's covenant of grace that would be established with Christ's blood. Each of the gospel writers makes note of the prophecies concerning John the Baptist (Matthew 3: 3; Mark 1: 3; Luke 3: 4; John 1: 23). He was a man sent by God to prepare the Jewish nation for the long-awaited Messiah.

Unlike the ministries of Jesus and the apostles, there is no record of John the Baptist performing miracles. He lived in the wilderness, ate locusts and honey, and wore clothing made of camel's hair (Matthew 3: 4). From this description, it is evident that people were not drawn to John because of his attractive lifestyle. What drew people to John? It was the message he delivered. John spoke in anticipation of the Messiah (Matthew 3: 11-12). His compelling presentation of that message was powerful enough to attract throngs of people who accepted his teaching and submitted to his baptism.

John's ministry was threefold in nature. First, he focused on repentance. While repentance was taught in the Old Testament, John's message was fresh as he proclaimed to the people, "Repent, for the kingdom of heaven is at hand" (Matthew 3: 2). He preached of repentance with urgency. Unlike Jonah who preached repentance as an opportunity to escape destruction (Jonah 3: 1-10), John preached repentance as a matter of hope. The Jews of John's time were on the precipice of a powerful spiritual journey. He taught repentance so that they might prepare themselves spiritually for the coming kingdom.

Once one believes in Jesus' sacrifice as God's mechanism of salvation, repentance is the first step in righting his/her relationship with God. Without repentance, a person cannot reach the spiritual plane that allows communion with God. Paul told the Corinthians, in teaching them about repentance:

> [9] I now rejoice, not that you were made sorrowful, but that you were made sorrowful to *the point of* repentance; for you were made sorrowful according to *the will of* God, so that you might not suffer loss in anything through us. [10] For the sorrow that is according to *the will of* God produces a repentance without regret, *leading* to salvation, but the sorrow of the world produces death. [11] For behold what earnestness this very thing, this godly sorrow, has produced in you: what vindication of yourselves, what indignation, what fear, what longing, what zeal, what avenging of wrong! (2 Corinthians 7: 9-11a)

Paul wrote of the same repentance about which John the Baptist preached. He taught the people of a repentance that reflected godly sorrow. What is godly sorrow? It is what one experiences when he/she understands sin from God's perspective – seeing sin as God sees sin. Paul wrote about someone reaching the point where he realizes how his sins have grieved God and the degree of disappointment it brings to him. Godly sorrow occurs when a person shares in God's grief over sins.

John the Baptist's ministry marked the beginning of a transition to the covenant of grace. In the Sermon on the Mount, Jesus explained that a relationship with God must be grounded in righteousness rather than the law. He taught that the Abrahamic covenant would see fulfillment in the covenant of grace (Matthew 5: 17). Paul complemented his words, telling the Romans that the seed of Abraham would now be a spiritual seed and people would be born into the new covenant as children of promise (Romans 9: 6-8).

The repentance John preached was accompanied by baptism (immersion in water) as the Jews began to accept the teaching of the coming kingdom. This was the second focus of his ministry. Why did John baptize? The short answer is that he was directed by God to baptize those who repented of their sins. Scripture states explicitly that it was God who sent John (John 1: 6). It also indicates that God sent him *to baptize*. That is the powerful message in the following verse.

> ...He who sent me to baptize in water said to me, 'He upon whom you see the Spirit descending and remaining upon Him, this is the One who baptizes in the Holy Spirit.' (John 1: 33)

This verse, when read in conjunction with John 1: 6, serves as witness that it was God who sent John to baptize. Also, the third focus of John's ministry comes to light here. He was sent to prepare the people for the coming Messiah and the kingdom he was about to introduce. He used assorted phrases to describe the coming savior. For instance, in this verse he identified Jesus as "the One who baptizes with the Holy Spirit." Matthew records John telling his listeners that "...He who is coming after me is mightier than I, and I am not fit to remove His sandals" (Matthew 3: 11). When Jesus approached John to receive baptism, John responded, "...I have need to be baptized by You, and do You come to me?" (Matthew 3: 14).

The preparatory nature of John's ministry had been prophesied in the Old Testament (Isaiah 40: 3; Malachi 3: 1). Thus, it stands to reason that the repentance he taught and the baptism he practiced were as anticipatory as his teaching about the coming Messiah. The repentance and baptism of John's ministry were intended to prepare people for repentance and baptism in the covenant of grace. The New Testament authors do not offer a lot of details about the life of John the Baptist, but the threefold character of his mission is well-displayed in the gospels. He came to prepare the Jews for what was to come.

The Nature of John's Baptism

John's life as God's messenger concerning the coming Messiah was prophesied by God-ordained prophets. This fact testifies to God's endorsement and oversight. According to Luke, it was God's desire for the Jews to submit to John's baptism (Luke 7: 30). John baptized because that was the direction he received from God. The real question to be answered is: *Why did God send John to baptize?* Exactly what purpose did baptism serve?

> John the Baptist appeared in the wilderness preaching a baptism of repentance for the forgiveness of sins. (Mark 1: 4)

> And he came into all the district around the Jordan, preaching a baptism of repentance for the forgiveness of sins. (Luke 3: 3)

Mark and Luke both state that John the Baptist preached *a baptism of repentance for the forgiveness of sins*. This depiction of John's ministry, and particularly the baptism he offered, has been a source of confusion for many since the English translation seems a bit awkward. Exactly what does *baptism of repentance* mean? Relatively few Bible commentators have spent much energy addressing the curious phrasing directly, presumably because the English rendering seems odd. Still, here are a couple of comments that might help provide some insight.

> baptism characterized by repentance[44]

> Baptism is here called, the baptism of repentance: because John required repentance antecedent to it, and administered it upon profession of repentance, and as an open testification of it.[45]

Perhaps the best explanation of the baptism that John offered is that it was baptism born of repentance. Listening to John's preaching, many were convicted of their sins and experienced the kind of godly sorrow previously discussed. In John's preaching, he not only called for repentance, but he also called upon those who repented to submit to baptism so the sins that weighed on them might be forgiven. It was *baptism of repentance for the forgiveness of sins*. Baptism, then, was a natural step for one who sought to follow John's teaching and right his/her relationship with God. In that sense, repentance begets baptism.

The term *baptism of repentance* may carry even deeper significance. The phrase could very well speak to the limitations of John's baptism in that it was *only* a baptism of repentance. Each time John's baptism is compared with the coming baptism of the church age, the baptism of John is portrayed as less significant (cf. Matthew 3: 11). When Paul met some disciples in Ephesus who had received the baptism of John, he told them, "John baptized with the baptism of repentance, telling the people to believe in Him who was coming after him, that is, in Jesus" (Acts 19: 4). He then baptized them in Jesus' name.

The baptism John performed did not have equal footing with baptism in Jesus' name since the blood from which Christian baptism draws its significance had not yet been spilled (cf. Matthew 26: 28). The new covenant would not become effective until Jesus' blood was shed.

---

[44] Constable, Thomas, *Expository Notes of Dr. Thomas Constable*, https://www.studylight.org/commentaries/dcc/john-3.html, accessed July 15, 2017.
[45] Gill, John, *Gill's Exposition of the Entire Bible*, http://biblehub.com/mark/1-4.htm, accessed August 10, 2017.

Scripture portrays the Day of Pentecost as the time the Holy Spirit ushered in the new covenant (Acts 2: 1-42) and the baptism of John was supplanted with baptism in Jesus' name (Acts 2: 38).

John's Baptism and John 3

Jesus told Nicodemus "…unless one is born again he cannot see the kingdom of God" (John 3: 3). He then reiterated, "…unless one is born of water and the Spirit he cannot enter into the kingdom of God" (John 3: 5). It is clear from the text, and scholars agree, that to be born again is to be born of water and the Spirit. Since the expression *born of water* does not serve as a reference to human childbirth, God's Word, or the Holy Spirit, the possibilities for the meaning of this phrase have become limited.

Some have proposed, and others have vehemently rejected, the idea that *born of water* was intended to point Nicodemus to the baptism taught and performed by John the Baptist. The water of the passage is in line with John's baptism since Scripture states repeatedly that John baptized with water (Matthew 3: 11; Mark 1: 8; Luke 3: 16; Acts 1: 5; 11: 16). Could it be that Jesus was telling Nicodemus that he must receive the baptism offered by John the Baptist in order to attain salvation and enter the kingdom of heaven?

There is solid biblical rationale behind the belief that Jesus may have been directing Nicodemus to the baptism of John, but it can also be argued that there are a couple of obstacles to this line of reasoning. If Jesus' remarks to Nicodemus were intended to indicate John's baptism, then these disparities must be reconciled.

The first obstacle to concluding that Jesus was speaking to Nicodemus of John's baptism is that at no other point in Scripture is John's baptism specifically defined as a means for attaining salvation. However, while God's Word does not specifically link salvation to John's baptism, there is an indirect biblical connection between the two. When addressing forgiveness of sins on and after the Day of Pentecost (cf. Acts 2: 38; 26: 18), Scripture links redemption with forgiveness. Therefore, to speak of forgiveness is to speak of redemption. This truth is made clear in the following verses from Paul's epistles.

> In Him we have redemption through His blood, the forgiveness of our trespasses, according to the riches of His grace. (Ephesians 1: 7)

> [13]For He rescued us from the domain of darkness, and transferred us to the kingdom of His beloved Son, [14] in whom we have redemption, the forgiveness of sins. (Colossians 1: 13-14)

Redemption is found in forgiveness of sins through Christ's blood. Upon receiving forgiveness/redemption, men are transferred to the Son of God's kingdom. These verses demonstrate that participation in the kingdom requires forgiveness of sins as a matter of redemption. It stands to reason, then, that entrance into the kingdom of heaven is granted through forgiveness of sins. This ties in nicely with John's baptism since it was "...baptism of repentance for the forgiveness of sins" (Mark 1: 4).

Given Paul's words of instruction in his epistles, it can be reasoned that the connection between John's baptism and forgiveness also provides a connection between John's baptism, redemption/salvation, and entrance into the kingdom. Jesus could forgive sins while on earth (Mark 2: 10). Forgiveness was also available through the God-ordained baptism performed by John. However, John's baptism was not intended as a permanent measure, partly because it was limited in scope – focused on the pre-Pentecost Jewish nation. It seems, however, that provisional forgiveness/redemption might be received through the baptism offered by John the Baptist with a view toward the coming kingdom. Those who received the baptism of John were later baptized in Jesus' name when Christian baptism became available (Acts 19: 1-7).

The second matter that seems problematic in linking John's baptism to John 3: 5 is that Jesus told Nicodemus he must be *born of water and the Spirit*. This indicates that birth of water as a matter of entering the kingdom involves the Holy Spirit. Yet, Scripture teaches that the Spirit was not yet available to men when these two met. The Spirit would not be given until after Jesus' ascension (John 7: 39). Since Jesus spoke with Nicodemus before he had been crucified on the cross, it is clear the Spirit was not yet given.

Most scholars seem to presume that when Jesus spoke of being born of the Spirit, he had in view the indwelling of the Holy Spirit taught by the apostles (Acts 2: 38; Romans 8: 9; 1 Corinthians 3: 16). However, the Spirit abiding in someone who has been reborn does not speak to the moment of rebirth, but to the new life that is lived after one has experienced rebirth. Consequently, Jesus may well have been referring to what happens at the time of one's spiritual birth.

The Holy Spirit has not one, but two distinct roles in connection with the new life of a convert. Most are familiar with his indwelling presence.

Peter pointed to the gift of the Holy Spirit that believers would receive once they had repented and submitted to baptism in Jesus' name (Acts 2: 38). That gift is addressed throughout the New Testament. Upon conversion, the Holy Spirit takes up spiritual residence within the new convert. Thus, believers are called God's temple (1 Corinthians 6: 19). However, the Holy Spirit has an additional role that gets far less attention.

The Holy Spirit is the member of the Godhead who is especially at work during one's submission to baptism. The work of regeneration belongs specifically to the Holy Spirit (Titus 3: 5). He does this work as Christ's blood is applied to sins as a cleansing agent, the believer is purified, and sins are forgiven (1 Peter 1: 2). Thus, being born of the Spirit logically points to the role of the Spirit during baptism. This explains why Jesus insisted that one must be born of water and the Spirit.

John's baptism was a matter of purification/forgiveness. This is demonstrated late in the third chapter of John's gospel where a dispute over purification focused on baptism (John 3: 25-26). However, John made it clear that the baptism he offered did not involve the Holy Spirit (Mark 1: 8). Since regeneration is the work of the Spirit, it can be reasoned that the regeneration linked to Christian baptism would not be available through John's baptism. This is another reason it was established as a temporary measure. Still, it would have served effectively as a transitional vessel prior to Jesus' death, introducing baptism as a time of forgiveness with a view to the kingdom.

Was John's baptism, or the baptism Jesus' disciples provided prior to his death (John 4: 1-2), necessary for one to know salvation? Since forgiveness and salvation go hand in hand, it can be argued that baptism and direct forgiveness by the Messiah might have a redemptive effect. Jesus could have forgiven Nicodemus of his sins, but he did not. Instead he pointed him to a birth of water and the Spirit – immersion in water – to enter the kingdom of God.

The first century was a world of limited communication. News of baptism would have spread mostly by word of mouth. Consequently, many would have lacked any knowledge of baptism. Yet, if Jesus was telling Nicodemus, at this early stage, that baptism was required for someone to enter the kingdom, it stands to reason that anyone who knew of baptism for the forgiveness of sins would likely be held to that standard.

Luke's narrative indicates that the Pharisees were held to a baptismal standard. Consequently, Jesus had good reason to speak with Nicodemus about baptism. Luke wrote that "...the Pharisees and the lawyers rejected God's purpose for themselves, not having been baptized by John" (Luke 7: 30). This statement indicates that they were not only aware of John's baptism, but they also understood God's expectation that they should submit to John's baptism. The text does not say that the Pharisees were blind to godly expectations or that they ignored godly expectations. Luke wrote that they repudiated (Gr. *ethetesan*) godly expectations. They could not "reject God's purpose for themselves" if they were not aware of that purpose.

Nicodemus did not ask what Jesus meant by the term *kingdom of God*. That is because, in John the Baptist's preaching, repentance and baptism were presented as a matter of introducing the coming kingdom. He preached repentance and baptism with the kingdom in view. The implication from the narrative is that John was saying, "Repent (and be baptized), for the kingdom of heaven is at hand" (Matthew 3: 2), denoting a link between repentance, baptism, and the kingdom. For those who heard John's message, including the Pharisees, that connection was clear.

Jews required baptism of those Gentiles who wished to convert to Judaism. Baptism was the vessel by which Gentiles (outsiders) could become part of something special (the Abrahamic covenant). Jews were born into their covenant with God. However, a Gentile could not be naturally born into the covenant. He could not enter a second time into his mother's womb and be born. Even if he could, he would still come out a Gentile. Therefore, baptism was designed as a figure (type) of childbirth as a matter of entrance into the covenant. This begs the question: *Why would the Pharisees reject John's baptism?*

Had the Pharisees submitted to John's baptism, it would have indicated to the Jews that, in the same way Gentiles were outsiders where the Abrahamic covenant was concerned, the Pharisees were outside the kingdom of heaven that John claimed was "at hand" (Matthew 3: 2). This would have suggested to the people that the Pharisees were not the elite religious leaders they claimed to be. That is why they despised the teaching and baptism of John. It exposed them for who they really were.

Born of God

The strongest biblical evidence that Jesus was, with the words *born of water and the Spirit*, directing Nicodemus toward John's baptism is found in the first chapter of the Apostle John's gospel. It is there that he introduced John the Baptist (John 1: 6-28). During that introduction, referring to Jesus as *the Light*, he identified the Baptist as the one who would "...testify about the Light" (John 1: 8). During his introduction of John the Baptist's ministry, the apostle penned the following words about the Messiah, of whom the Baptist was to serve as witness.

> [12] But as many as received Him, to them He gave the right to become children of God, *even* to those who believe in His name, [13] who were born, not of blood nor of the will of the flesh nor of the will of man, but of God. (John 1: 12-13)

The Holy Spirit is God (cf. Genesis 1: 2; Acts 5: 3-4; Romans 8: 14). This means that when someone is "...born of the Spirit" (John 3: 6), that person is "...born...of God" (v. 13), or "...born again" (John 3: 3). These phrases are interchangeable. Indeed, spiritual birth/rebirth is thematic in the first section of John's gospel (chapters 1-3). This *birth of God* is unquestionably the same *spiritual birth* Jesus later addressed with Nicodemus.

The parallel structure of the apostle's instructions concerning being born of God and Jesus' instructions about being born of water and the Spirit is too glaring to ignore. For instance, becoming a child of God (v. 12) naturally implies spiritual birth and intimates the same eternal objective as entering the kingdom (John 3: 5). Additionally, just as Jesus taught Nicodemus that entrance into the kingdom would be limited to those "...born of water and the Spirit" (John 3: 5), so the apostle explained that "...the right to become children of God" is limited to "as many as...were born...of God" (vv. 12-13). Finally, using words strikingly similar to those in Jesus' exchange with the Pharisee, the apostle contrasts being born of God against fleshly birth (v. 13). Thus, when Jesus told Nicodemus that he must be born of water and the Spirit, he was telling him he must be born of God.

These verses in the first chapter of John constitute what can be considered the expanded text surrounding John 3: 5 (see Preface, p. 7), Here the apostle has directly connected the idea of spiritual birth with the ministry of John the Baptist. This, it seems, was the intended result of his ministry – that people might be born of God. Since the focus of John's ministry was to 1) teach repentance, 2) baptize, and 3) prepare the people for the coming Messiah, it stands to reason that these were the tools he used to guide people to spiritual birth.

The Spirit-inspired authors of God's Word were meticulous in their development of a well-defined path of instruction for the Christian world to follow. Since the Apostle John twice wrote of spiritual birth in a confined section of Scripture, the connection between the two narratives is plain to see. John's introduction of the topic of spiritual birth (born of God) in the first chapter was undoubtedly intended to lay the groundwork for the ensuing conversation between Jesus and Nicodemus. Given this context, it is not unreasonable to see Jesus' directive to Nicodemus as a nod to the provisional baptism performed by John the Baptist, which the Pharisees had previously rejected. Still, there is one other option that must also be given honest consideration.

Chapter 6
- Born of Water -
Christian Baptism

Introducing Christian Baptism

The combination of repentance and baptism taught by John the Baptist was forward-looking. He did not seek disciples for himself, but for the one who would follow. Still, the *form* of baptism John practiced (immersion in water), would continue into the church age, but with some noteworthy changes. First, unlike John's baptism, Christian baptism would be administered *in Jesus' name.* Second, those in the church age receiving baptism could anticipate the Holy Spirit's intimate involvement in their lives (Acts 2: 38) – also known as the indwelling of the Holy Spirit (cf. Romans 8: 9).

When Jesus commanded his disciples to baptize, he told them, "…make disciples of all nations, baptizing them in the name of the Father and the Son and the Holy Spirit" (Matthew 28: 19). Yet, through the balance of the New Testament baptism is depicted as being performed *in Jesus' name* and some have wondered if this is significant. Since Scripture does not contradict itself, there must be a reasonable explanation for this distinction.

To do something in someone's name is to do it under the authority of that name. Christian baptism is performed in Jesus' name, which means it is done under his authority, and rightfully so since it was his blood that was shed. Many confuse *authority* with what may be considered a *formula of words*, suggesting that the specific phrasing *in Jesus' name* must accompany immersion and that anything else is not only unbiblical, but unacceptable to God. Yet, there is strong evidence from early church records that when an individual was baptized, the baptizer declared that they were being baptized in the name of the Father, the Son, and the Holy Spirit. This would be in keeping with Jesus' instructions.

In Scripture, when the apostles and others taught baptism in Jesus' name (e.g., Acts 2: 38; 10: 48; 19: 4-5; 22: 16; 1 Corinthians 6: 11), they had in view the authority with which baptism was given. They were not speaking or writing about specific terminology that was meant to accompany baptism in order to validate the ceremony. According to Scripture, everything believers do is to be done in Jesus' name (Colossians 3: 17), so the expression is not about restrictive wording, but about perspective.

Submission to baptism is submission to Christ and his authority. It is a matter of identifying with him. When the Israelites "...were baptized into Moses" (1 Corinthians 10: 2) they identified with him. Similarly, Paul told the Corinthians it was foolish to think they might belong to an imaginary segment of Christianity led by Paul. He was not crucified for them and they had not been baptized in the name of Paul (1 Corinthians 1: 13). Rather, in their baptism they identified with Jesus in whose name and under whose authority baptism was given.

Baptism in the name of the Father, the Son, and the Holy Spirit does not contradict the biblical teaching that baptism is to be performed in Jesus' name. In fact, it was Jesus who commanded baptism in the name of the Father, the Son, and the Holy Spirit and he had the authority to determine how baptism in his name would be carried out. This is the baptism of Scripture that Jesus authorized; therefore, it is administered under his authority, or in his name.

The Role of Christian Baptism

One of the greatest doctrinal disputes among Christendom in modern times focuses on the role of baptism in the church age. The debate seems odd since Scripture is remarkably straightforward in its presentation of baptism's redemptive character. Despite the forthrightness of Scripture, seemingly countless arguments have been offered to challenge biblical instruction on baptism.

Many reject the portrayal of baptism as a redemptive matter, insisting that it is a meritorious work and salvation cannot be earned. Consequently, when faced with passages of Scripture that present baptism as a salvific matter, of which there are many, those passages must be explained away. Numerous methods have been developed over the past few centuries to deal with the many passages that speak of baptism. Generally, men insist that a passage does not *mean* what it says or does not *say* what it says.

The claim by the evangelical community that baptism is a meritorious work defies biblical reason. In his letter to Titus, Paul specifically contrasts baptism and works (Titus 3: 5). Also, baptism is not something one does (in an active sense). It is something to which one submits. The phrase *be baptized* is passive, respecting the fact that it is not a deed of merit, but an act of humility. It is a rite of passage designed by God for those who seek him.

Like John's baptism, Christian baptism is for forgiveness of sins. This was made clear on the Day of Pentecost when, in answer to the plea from the crowd, "…what shall we do?" (Acts 2: 37), Peter responded, telling the people, "Repent, and each of you be baptized in the name of Jesus Christ for the forgiveness of your sins; and you will receive the gift of the Holy Spirit" (Acts 2: 38). This same connection between Christian baptism and forgiveness is repeated elsewhere in God's Word (Acts 22: 16; Romans 6: 1-4; Colossians 2: 11-14).

Baptism identifies one with Christ. This was Paul's point in his letter to the Corinthians (1 Corinthians 1: 11-15). In like fashion, he told the Galatians that they had *clothed* themselves with Christ when they were baptized, taking on the identity of Christ (Galatians 3: 27). Paul also told the Corinthians that in baptism they had become a part of the body of Christ, which is the church (1 Corinthians 12: 13).

Baptism is consistently portrayed in Scripture as the moment when one is transformed from being outside of Christ to one who has taken on the Christian identity. It is described as a critical matter where salvation is concerned (Mark 16: 16; Acts 2: 38; 1 Peter 3: 21). Baptism is the defining moment for one who seeks to accept Jesus as Savior. There is no reason to believe that these passages do not *say* what they say and *mean* what they say. The arguments against this are too weak, too forced, and were developed far too late (by centuries) to withstand biblical scrutiny.

Availability of Christian Baptism

Where John 3: 5 is concerned, many have made a seemingly legitimate point noting that Christian baptism (in Jesus' name) was not yet available when Jesus spoke to Nicodemus. It was not made available until the Day of Pentecost (Acts 2: 38), weeks after Jesus' death and resurrection. Consequently, it is said, Jesus could not have had Christian baptism in view in his conversation with Nicodemus. It is then argued that Jesus had in mind *baptism with the Holy Spirit* – a baptism that presumably involved the Holy Spirit, but not water – as prophesied by John the Baptist when he said:

> I baptized you with water; but He will baptize you with the Holy Spirit. (Mark 1: 8)

The difficulty with this line of reasoning, which was discussed earlier, is that the Holy Spirit would not be given until Jesus was glorified (John 7: 39). The Spirit was given to the disciples on a limited basis prior to Jesus' death (John 20: 22). However, just as Christian baptism was introduced on the Day of Pentecost, so the Spirit was first offered universally on that day. Therefore, if Jesus could not have been speaking to Nicodemus about Christian immersion in water because it was not yet available, the same principle would apply where baptism with the Holy Spirit was concerned.

Jesus spoke frequently of the coming kingdom. Many of his parables begin with the words *the kingdom of heaven is like*. In the Sermon on the Mount, the expression *kingdom of heaven* appears six times and in Matthew's gospel this phrase appears a total of twenty-five times. In the four gospels, the term *kingdom of God* is found forty-six times. It seems then, that presenting the coming kingdom to the Jews was Jesus' focus. This would have been equally true in his visit with Nicodemus. D. A. Carson makes this point well, explaining:

> If we take the Gospel records seriously, we must conclude that Jesus sometimes proclaimed truth the full significance and application of which could be fully appreciated and experienced only after he had risen from the dead. John 3 falls under this category.[46]

Jesus often used figurative language to make his point. His words in the following passage appear later in John's gospel. Jesus seemed to be discussing issues that could only have meaning in the coming church age.

> [53] So Jesus said to them, 'Truly, truly, I say to you, unless you eat the flesh of the Son of Man and drink His blood, you have no life in yourselves. [54] He who eats My flesh and drinks My blood has eternal life, and I will raise him up on the last day. [55] For My flesh is true food, and My blood is true drink.

---

[46] Carson, D. A., *D.A. Carson on the meaning of "born of water and of the Spirit"* https://aaronshaf.wordpress.com/2011/12/21/d-a-carson-on-the-meaning-of-born-of-water-and-of-the-spirit/, accessed August 23, 2017.

[56] He who eats My flesh and drinks My blood abides in Me, and I in him.' (John 6: 53-56)

While it can be reasonably argued that the text holds an early allusion to the Lord's Supper, which had not yet been introduced, the larger lesson is that salvation is available only through Christ's sacrifice of himself. Yet, no one would have spiritual access to Jesus' flesh and blood until after his death, burial, and resurrection. In truth, nothing about this passage could apply at the time these words were spoken. Jesus was speaking of truths not yet known to men.

Similarly, in John 3: 5, *born of water* harmonizes fully with later passages that discuss the role of Christian baptism. The fact that something was unknown at the time did not prevent Jesus from offering a preview of what was to come.

Men and Their Words

It is fascinating the lengths to which men will go to divorce baptism from salvation including some renowned theologians. For instance, when dealing with certain verses, A. T. Robertson (1863-1934) unknowingly stumbled over his own words, figuratively speaking. The following words were spoken by Jesus as he offered his disciples the cup of communion.

> ...for this is My blood of the covenant, which is poured out for many for forgiveness of sins. (Matthew 26: 28)

Make note of the Greek phrase *eis aphesin hamartion*, which is translated *for forgiveness of sins*. It is the same phrase that defined the baptism of John the Baptist as he administered *baptism of repentance for the forgiveness of sins*. Concerning this phrase, Robertson wrote:

> This clause is in Matthew alone but it is not to be restricted for that reason. It is the truth. This passage answers all the modern sentimentalism that finds in the teaching of Jesus only pious ethical remarks or eschatological dreamings. He had the definite conception of his death on the cross as the basis of forgiveness of sin. The purpose of the shedding of his blood of the New Covenant was precisely to remove (forgive) sins.[47]

---

[47] Robertson, A. T., *Robertson's Word Pictures of the New Testament*, https://www.studylight.org/commentaries/rwp/matthew-26.html, accessed August 12, 2017.

Mr. Robertson wrote that the phrase *for forgiveness of sins* is found "...in Matthew alone." He seems to have overlooked the fact that this same expression also appears in Mark 1: 4, Luke 3: 3; 24: 47, and Acts 2: 38. The first two passages concern John's baptism and the second Luke passage speaks to repentance for forgiveness of sins based on Christ's sacrifice that was to be preached. Acts 2: 38 is part of Peter's sermon from the Day of Pentecost where, again, baptism is in view.

In Peter's sermon, while some Greek texts read *eis aphesin ton hamartion hymon*, which translated means *for the forgiveness of sins of you*, most omit the prepositional phrase *of you* and read exactly as the phrase appears in Matthew. In Jesus' words to the disciples, Mr. Robertson recognized that *for forgiveness of sins* identifies the purpose for which Jesus shed his blood. How did he understand these same words when spoken by Peter on the Day of Pentecost in connection with baptism?

> In themselves the words can express aim or purpose for that use of *eis* does exist ... One will decide the use here according as he believes that baptism is essential to the remission of sins or not. [48]

Mr. Robertson's comments on the same phrase as it appears in these two verses seem at odds. His definitive explanation of this phrase from the account in Matthew where *eis* represents purpose or goal is not equally reflected in his thoughts on Acts 2: 38. His treatment of this terminology in connection with John's baptism is comparable to his analysis in Acts. Similarly, where John 3: 5 is concerned, another popular theologian, John Gill, who was mentioned earlier, appears to have contradicted himself. Writing about John 3: 5, he penned the following explanation.

> ...by 'water', is not meant material water, or baptismal water; for water baptism is never expressed by water only, without some additional word, which shows, that the ordinance of water baptism is intended.[49]

It is unclear what additional word might satisfy Mr. Gill's condition for water to mean baptism. Consequently, his method for distinguishing between a statement where water means baptism and a statement where

---

[48] Robertson, A. T., *Robertson's Word Pictures of the New Testament*, https://www.studylight.org/commentaries/rwp/acts-2.html, accessed August 12, 2017.
[49] Gill, John, *Gill's Exposition of the Entire Bible*, http://biblehub.com/commentaries/gill/john/3.htm, accessed August 15, 2017.

it does not is vague. However, perusing his commentary, the reader soon discovers that Gill's rejection of a meaning of baptism in John 3: 5 is grounded in his belief that baptism has no "regenerating influence."[50] Therefore, on the surface his stated requirement of additional confirmation within the narrative seems suspect.

In the Apostle John's first epistle, he shared some thoughts about Christ's deity, telling his audience, "For there are three that testify: the Spirit and the water and the blood; and the three are in agreement" (1 John 5: 7-8). Unlike his comments about the water mentioned in Jesus' conversation with Nicodemus, Gill offered the following observation about the water John referenced in his epistle.

> By water is designed, not internal sanctification, which though an evidence of regeneration and adoption, yet not of Christ's sonship; but water baptism, as administered on earth in the name of the Father, and of the Son, and of the Holy Ghost.[51]

Again, there is inconsistency, this time in John Gill's writings. When Gill wrote about the water in John 3: 5, he insisted that "...water baptism is never expressed by water only, without some additional word, which shows, that the ordinance of water baptism is intended." Yet, no "additional word" is given in 1 John. Other than 1 John 5: 6-8 where *water* is mentioned four times, baptism is not discussed in this epistle. Yet, like other Bible scholars, John Gill recognized that water, in this instance, represents baptism. Add to this the fact that the same person, the Apostle John, penned both passages where water is identified with baptism. Perhaps John was even influenced by Jesus' words to Nicodemus when he referred to baptism as water in his epistle. Yet, according to John Gill, the apostle had two completely different ideas in view.

This is not an attempt to mock admired men like Robertson and Gill. The point is that even respected Bible scholars are known to approach the topic of baptism with a doctrinal bias that blinds them to the words of Scripture. If well-studied men like these could contradict themselves where baptism is concerned, it is no wonder that others who are not as

---

[50] Gill, John, *Gill's Exposition of the Entire Bible*, http://biblehub.com/commentaries/gill/john/3.htm, accessed August 15, 2017.
[51] Gill, John, *Gill's Exposition of the Entire Bible*, http://biblehub.com/commentaries/gill/1_john/5.htm, accessed August 15, 2017.

well-read might easily fall prey to the teachings of those whom they believe are better informed.

Entering the Kingdom

To what was Jesus pointing when he told Nicodemus he must be born again? What did he have in mind with the words *born of water and the Spirit*? This is the heart of the matter. Giving due consideration to biblical teaching on baptism, the reasonable conclusion is that Jesus was describing immersion in water.

Nicodemus knew John's baptism all too well as did other Pharisees. When Jesus told Nicodemus that one must be born of water and the Spirit to enter the kingdom, John's baptism would have come to mind for the Pharisee. It is reasonable to believe that those who were aware of John's baptism for the forgiveness of sins and rejected it would be held accountable for that decision. Given Jesus' words, it seems this would be enough to keep them from sharing in the kingdom since their sins would remain unremitted.

As with Jesus' lessons throughout his ministry, he spoke directly to his immediate audience (in this case it was Nicodemus), but he also spoke to all who would read his words in the coming church age. This leads to the conclusion that Jesus had in mind the significance of Christian baptism, portraying it as a matter of participation in the kingdom of heaven. This was the prevailing view in the church for the first fifteen hundred years after Jesus made this statement. It is in keeping with baptism instruction in the gospels, the book of Acts, and through the epistles.

What is baptism? What purpose does it serve? Baptism is the manner by which men access the grace of God through Christ's blood. Forgiveness is attained in baptism (Acts 2: 38; 22: 16; Colossians 2: 11-14). It is the appointed time when Jesus' blood is applied to one's sins (1 Peter 1: 2) and that person is reborn – entering the kingdom as a babe in Christ. This is what Jesus had in mind when he said, "...unless one is born of water and the Spirit, he cannot enter into the kingdom of God" (John 3: 5).

It could be reasonably argued, based on his classic work titled *Baptism in the New Testament*, that G. R. Beasley-Murray was as well-versed on the topic of baptism as any human being since the apostles. In that well-known treatise on baptism he wrote the following concerning John 3: 5.

...at a time when the employment of water for cleansing in view of the last day had taken the specific form of baptism, it is difficult to take seriously any other reference than baptism in the words εξ υδατος.[52]

R. C. Foster (1888-1970) was a prominent theologian of the twentieth century. He penned what could arguably be called the most comprehensive study ever written concerning the life of Christ. In that work Foster had much to say about the expression *born of water and the Spirit*. He summed up his exposition with the following remarks:

The reference to immersion is inescapable. In the act of baptism the whole man – body, mind, and soul – is buried and comes forth a new creature in Christ.[53]

When Jesus told Nicodemus that he must be born of water and the Spirit, the Pharisee would have naturally pictured John's baptism. Still, the prophecy John offered concerning an imminent baptism that would be more powerful than his own cannot be ignored. Therefore, John's baptism would have been in view only as an interim device during the period of transition to the covenant of grace.

Just as John functioned as the forerunner of Christ, the baptism he administered served as a herald of Christian baptism. The passage is ultimately aimed at those who live in the church age. Given the context of Jesus' words, only Christian immersion in water fully explains what it means to be born of water and the Spirit. This was Jesus' way of stating that he expects each one to be baptized in his name as a matter of spiritual renewal.

The Nicodemus Perspective

Over the past several centuries, men have sought to overcome the natural and powerful imagery of baptism that emanates from Jesus' words to Nicodemus. This has resulted in the doctrinal disparities discussed in this book. However, when it comes to determining an acceptable meaning of this verse, one cannot ignore Nicodemus's point of view. The true meaning of John 3: 5 will necessarily harmonize with the Pharisee's first century perspective.

---

[52] Beasely-Murray, G. R., *Baptism in the New Testament*, William B. Eerdman's Publishing Company, Grand Rapids, MI, 1973, pp 228-229.
[53] Foster, R. C., *Studies in the Life of Christ*, College Press Publishing Company, Joplin, MO., 1995, p. 371.

While modern men have suggested assorted meanings for *born of water* (i.e., childbirth, God's Word, or the Holy Spirit), it is difficult to imagine how Nicodemus could have come to any of those same conclusions. Nothing within the framework of the conversation or the context of the narrative leads down those paths, so it seems a considerable leap to suggest that Nicodemus might have so quickly settled on one of these answers.

Nicodemus's response to Jesus' directive is very telling. While the evangelical community maintains that the phrase *born of water* is confounding and can only be understood by drawing from other New Testament passages, Nicodemus did not seem to be confused by Jesus' words. Had he failed to understand, it can be reasonably inferred that he would have asked Jesus to explain himself just as he had inquired concerning the term *born again*. Yet, he did not ask what Jesus meant with this new phrasing. Instead, he asked, "How can these things be?" (v. 8). He wanted to know how being born of water and the Spirit fit into God's redemptive plan.

There are two reasons Nicodemus would have readily understood Jesus' words as a depiction of baptism. The first lies in the fact that the Pharisees were thoroughly acquainted with the teaching of John the Baptist. It is axiomatic that they believed one of their God-ordained roles was to keep a watchful eye on religious activity among the Jews. In what was evidently an attempt to know their enemy, they closely monitored this wilderness preacher who had captured the attention of their constituents. Comparable scrutiny of Jesus explains why Nicodemus was familiar with him and his ministry.

John's ministry, the baptisms he performed, and the prophecies he offered, were at the forefront of Jewish conversation at the time. In their discourse, Jesus painted for Nicodemus a compelling portrait of John's prophecy concerning baptism with the Holy Spirit (Mark 1: 8), confident that a Pharisee would know exactly what he meant.

The second reason Nicodemus found it unnecessary to question Jesus' meaning is that he was not distracted by other New Testament passages that are often used to "...shout baptism out of this passage"[54] as Coffman observed. The books of Ephesians, James, 1 Peter, and even the gospel of John, from which others have forged their various meanings for born of water, were not yet written at the time of this conversation. Additionally, it would be centuries before the Greek *kai*

---

[54] Coffman, John, *Coffman's Commentaries on the Bible - John*, A.C.U Press, Abilene, TX, 1974, p. 84.

would be translated into the King James Version of the Bible, prompting yet another strategy to erase baptism from the text. Therefore, any meaning Nicodemus derived from Jesus' words must have been drawn from the conversation itself in combination with what he already knew.

The Apostle John, recording the exchange between Jesus and Nicodemus, does not mention a prolonged pause by the Pharisee that he might contemplate the term *born of water*. There may have been momentary silence between Jesus' words and Nicodemus's response; however, in that moment, the Pharisee could not have employed the labored reasoning offered by modern-day theologians to determine Jesus' meaning. He did not have the resources to devise an intricate doctrinal path leading away from baptism.

The only information Nicodemus had available that could have any bearing on this conversation is what he knew of John's and Jesus' ministries at the time. For instance, he would have known about John's emphasis on repentance and baptism (Matthew 3: 11; Mark 1: 4). It is reasonable to believe he knew of John's prophecy about baptism and the coming Messiah (Mark 1: 8). He was certainly cognizant of Jesus' connection with John the Baptist (Luke 1: 39-45; John 1: 29-34). Additionally, Nicodemus understood that Jesus was sent from God (John 3: 2). Finally, during their conversation, he learned of Jesus' insistence that one must be "…born again" (John 3: 3), or "…born of water and the Spirit" (John 3: 5), to participate in God's kingdom. This is the information that would have influenced his reasoning at the time.

Nicodemus could not have known what men like James, John, Peter, and Paul would write decades down the road, much less draw a connection between their words and the phrase *born of water*. He could not have known that, nearly two millennia later, someone would propose translating the Greek conjunction *kai* into English as an adverb. These arguments fail the *reasonableness* test and must, therefore, yield to evenhanded biblical analysis. When sound hermeneutic principles are applied to John 3: 5, it becomes evident that Nicodemus would have understood Jesus' words as a depiction of the rite of baptism.

Chapter 7

Baptism in Church History

Baptism and the Early Church

At the end of the first century, while many of the books/letters of Scripture were well-circulated, the formalization and canonization of the Bible was not yet complete. With the passing of the apostles, the teaching and well-being of the church was left to those who had learned directly from the lips of the apostles. These men in turn passed their knowledge to the next generation of church leaders who then passed it to the next. Those who lived in the first century, learned from the apostles, and worked beside them, are referred to historically as Apostolic Fathers because of that connection.

The men who learned from and succeeded the Apostolic Fathers in church leadership are known as Early Church Fathers. This group is categorized by their proximity to the Nicene Council that took place in AD 325. Those who predate the Nicene Council are known as Ante-Nicene Fathers and those who lived during and after this Council are called Nicene and Post-Nicene Fathers respectively.

It is important to remember that the Apostolic and Early Church Fathers were not apostles. They were not commissioned by Jesus to an apostolic ministry and their writings should not be considered Spirit-inspired. In fact, there are times when their views failed to harmonize with the lessons of Scripture. Still, where these men were unified in their understanding of apostolic instruction it is possible to gain considerable insight into the early church's perspective on certain topics.

Apostolic Fathers

Few writings of the Apostolic Fathers have survived the centuries, but those that have survived are filled with valuable insights into the teachings of the apostles. There are some modern theologians who insist that certain works attributed to the Apostolic Fathers are not original, and this is very possible since many counterfeiters came on the scene in the early stages of the church. Still, sufficient information is available to determine certain truths from their writings.

Most will recall the name Barnabas. He was Paul's traveling companion. According to Luke, he was a Levite by the name of Joseph "…who was also called Barnabas by the apostles (which translated means Son of Encouragement)" (Acts 4: 36). He was the one who introduced the converted Paul to the apostles in Jerusalem (Acts 9: 27). While they had their differences, Scripture portrays Barnabas as Paul's close friend.

It is often contended by modern theologians that Paul, in his ministry, sought to de-emphasize the significance of baptism with statements like the following:

> [14] I thank God that I baptized none of you … [17] For Christ did not send me to baptize, but to preach the gospel… (1 Corinthians 1: 14a, 17a)

> For by grace you have been saved through faith; and that not of yourselves, *it is* the gift of God. (Ephesians 2: 8)

When context is considered, it becomes clear that Paul was not seeking to minimize baptism with these words. Barnabas, a man who spent considerable time with Paul preaching the gospel message, would have undoubtedly recognized that Paul was dissociating baptism from salvation if that was the case. However, these excerpts from *The Epistle of Barnabas* suggest something different.

> Let us inquire, therefore, if the Lord cared to show us beforehand concerning the water and concerning the cross. Concerning the water it is written, with respect to Israel, how that they will not receive the baptism that bringeth remission of sins, but will establish one for themselves. [55]

> Blessed are they who having hoped on the cross have gone down into the water. For he speaketh of a reward to be given at the due season; then, saith

---

[55] Barnabas, *The Epistle of Barnabas* 11: 1, Early Christian Writings, http://www.earlychristianwritings.com/text/barnabas-hoole.html, accessed August 30, 2017.

he, I will render what is due unto you. But now in that he saith, Their leaves shall not fall off, he meaneth this, That every word that goeth out from your mouth in faith and love shall be for a refuge and a hope unto many… By this he meaneth that we go down into the water full of sin and pollution, and go up bearing fruit in the heart, having in the spirit fear and hope toward Jesus. And whoever shall eat of them shall live for ever. He meaneth this, Whoever, he saith, shall hear these words spoken and believe them shall live for ever. [56]

If Paul sought to diminish the significance of baptism in his teaching, these writings from Barnabas indicate that he was unaffected. Considering Barnabas's words, it is difficult to understand how he and Paul might have developed such a chasm in their views on baptism. Then again, perhaps they were not so different. After all, Paul did write the following:

Therefore we have been buried with Him through baptism into death, so that as Christ was raised from the dead through the glory of the Father, so we too might walk in newness of life. (Romans 6: 4)

For by one Spirit we were all baptized into one body, whether Jews or Greeks, whether slaves or free, and we were all made to drink of one Spirit. (1 Corinthians 12: 13)

For all of you who were baptized into Christ have clothed yourselves with Christ. (Galatians 3: 27)

[4] *There is* one body and one Spirit, just as also you were called in one hope of your calling; [5] one Lord, one faith, one baptism, [6] one God and Father of all who is over all and through all and in all. (Ephesians 4: 4-6)

Clement of Rome was a student/friend of both Peter and Paul. It is believed that this is the Clement mentioned by Paul in Philippians 4: 3. Tradition has it that Clement was martyred for his beliefs around the year AD 100, being tossed into the sea tied to an anchor. Treating baptism with the utmost care and respect, he wrote in *2 Clement*:

With what confidence shall we enter into the royal house of God if we do not keep our baptism pure and undefiled? Or who will be our advocate if we are not found to have holy righteous works?[57]

---

[56] Barnabas, *The Epistle of Barnabas* 11: 8 & 11, Early Christian Writings http://www.earlychristianwritings.com/text/barnabas-hoole.html, accessed August 30, 2017.
[57] Ferguson, Everett, *Baptism in the Early Church*, citing Clement of Rome, William B. Eerdman Publishing Company, Grand Rapids, MI, 2009, p. 207.

In what sense did Clement mean that baptism must be kept "pure and undefiled?" If submission to baptism is the manner by which sins are forgiven, it stands to reason that keeping baptism *pure* means that, once an individual's sins are forgiven, he/she must change moral direction and live a life of virtue rather than a life of sin, respecting the forgiveness God has granted.

One of the better-known students of the apostles was a man named Ignatius. It is unknown exactly when he was born and when he died, although there is some evidence that he died somewhere around A.D. 110 between the ages of 75 and 85. Known as Ignatius of Antioch, he was a student of the Apostle John and may have done some studying under Paul. During his final journey to Rome, which ended in his martyrdom, he wrote several letters to churches and individuals. In *The Epistle of Ignatius to the Trallians* is written:

> Wherefore also, ye appear to me to live not after the manner of men, but according to Jesus Christ, who died for us, in order that, by believing in His death, ye may by baptism be made partakers of His resurrection.[58]

In this letter, Ignatius states plainly that baptism is the very means by which believers are, "...made partakers of His resurrection." This is similar to Paul's explanations to the Romans and Colossians about baptism in the church age (Romans 6: 1-22; Colossians 2: 11-12). It also fits nicely with Jesus' words to Nicodemus that one must be born of water and the Spirit to enter the kingdom.

A man named Hermas lived in Rome and was among those to whom Paul wrote salutations in the lengthy conclusion of his letter to the church there (Romans 16: 14). Many presume this was the same Hermas responsible for the authorship of a document titled *The Shepherd of Hermas* late in the first century. Others believe it may have been written by a young contemporary of Clement of Rome. Some scholars like Graydon Snyder and A. D. Howel-Smith believe the work was written later – perhaps in the second century – suggesting that Hermas of Rome was not the author. This view, it is argued, is supported by the Muratorian Canon, an ancient list of canonical books developed late in the second century.

---

[58] Ignatius, *Epistle of Ignatius to the Trallians*, Chapter II, Early Christian Writings, http://www.earlychristianwritings.com/text/ignatius-trallians-longer.html, accessed August 28, 2017.

The Shepherd of Hermas is an allegorical work, so much that is written there is figurative. Still, the work was extremely popular in the early stages of the church, was considered a candidate for canonization, and appeared in the Sinaitic Codex – a trusted Greek manuscript of New Testament works. While the work is allegorical, no one doubts that it faithfully reflects the moral and theological views of the early church. With that in mind, the following conversation is documented within the pages of this work.

> "I have heard, Sir," say I, "from certain teachers, that there is no other repentance, save that which took place when we went down into the water and obtained remission of our former sins. He saith to me; "Thou hast well heard; for so it is."[59]

Ante-Nicene Fathers

Following the Apostolic Fathers were their students who are known as the Ante-Nicene Fathers. One of the better-known of these Early Church Fathers is a man by the name of Justin Martyr (A.D. 100-165). He was generally well-versed, having studied with Stoics, Aristotelians, Pythagoreans, and Platonists. It is said that Martyr was fascinated by the conviction of Christian martyrs, which is what led him to Christ. He gave his own life for his beliefs when he was beheaded in A.D. 165.

Justin Martyr wrote prolifically, but only a few documents have survived. These include *The First Apology*; *The Second Apology*; *The Dialogue with Trypho*; and *Constitutions of the Holy Apostles*. In *The First Apology*, and later in *The Dialogue with Trypho*, Justin Martyr addressed the topic of baptism at length, writing:

> As many as are persuaded and believe that what we teach and say is true, and undertake to be able to live accordingly, are instructed to pray and to entreat God with fasting, for the remission of their sins that are past, we praying and fasting with them. Then they are brought by us where there is water, and are regenerated in the same manner in which we were ourselves regenerated. For, in the name of God, the Father and Lord of the universe, and of our Savior Jesus Christ, and of the Holy Spirit, they then receive the washing with water. For Christ also said, 'Except ye be born again, ye shall not enter into the kingdom of heaven.' Now, that it is impossible for those who have once been born to enter into their mothers' wombs, is manifest to all...And for this we have learned from the apostles this reason. Since at our birth we were born

---

[59] Hermas, *Shepherd of Hermas*, Early Christian Writings, http://www.earlychristianwritings.com/text/shepherd-lightfoot.html, accessed August 30, 2017.

without our own knowledge or choice, by our parents coming together, and were brought up in bad habits and wicked training; in order that we may not remain the children of necessity and of ignorance, but may become the children of choice and knowledge, and may obtain in the water the remission of sins formerly committed, there is pronounced over him who chooses to be born again, and has repented of his sins, the name of God the Father and Lord of the universe.[60]

The Constitutions of the Holy Apostles also refers to John 3:5. There, the one who refuses to be baptized is to be condemned as an unbeliever, partially on the basis of what Jesus told Nicodemus:

'He that, out of contempt, will not be baptized, shall be condemned as an unbeliever, and shall be reproached as ungrateful and foolish. For the Lord says: 'Except a man be baptized of water and of the Spirit, he shall by no means enter into the kingdom of heaven.' And again: 'He that believeth and is baptized shall be saved but he that believeth not shall be damned.' [61]

As with other Early Church Fathers, Justin Martyr not only understood, but also wrote that one's regeneration takes place at the time of baptism. He also repeatedly recognized that, where John 3: 5 is concerned, Jesus was telling Nicodemus that one must be baptized as a matter of redemption. The connection between baptism and being born again is pointedly demonstrated in Justin Martyr's words.

Irenaeus (A.D. 120-205), like Justin Martyr, was a second century church leader. He studied under Polycarp, who was a student and friend of the Apostle John who recorded the conversation between Jesus and Nicodemus. Irenaeus's confidence that the expression *born of water* serves as a depiction of baptism suggests that Polycarp, his mentor, may well have shared insights he had received from the apostle concerning that passage of Scripture.

As we are lepers in sin, we are made clean from our old transgressions by means of the sacred water and the invocation of the Lord. We are thus spiritually regenerated as newborn infants, even as the Lord has declared: 'Except a man be born again through water and the Spirit, he shall not enter into the kingdom of heaven.'[62]

---

[60] Martyr, Justin, *First Apology*, http://www.newadvent.org/fathers/0126.htm., accessed September 23, 2017.

[61] Martyr, Justin, *Constitutions of the Holy Apostles*, http://www.bible.ca/H-baptism.htm, accessed September 23, 2017.

[62] Irenaeus, *Fragments From Lost Writings, No. 34*, http://www.newadvent.org/fathers/0134.htm, accessed September 3, 2017.

> This class of men have been instigated by Satan to a denial of that baptism which is regeneration to God, and thus to a renunciation of the whole faith.[63]

Tertullian (est. A.D. 155-240) was a third-generation church leader born in the middle of the second century. He is best remembered for writing *On Baptism*, the oldest surviving treatise dedicated solely to the topic of baptism. In that work Tertullian noted:

> ...the act of baptism itself too is carnal, in that we are plunged in water, but the effect spiritual, in that we are freed from sins.[64]

Cyprian of Carthage (A.D. 200-258) was a younger contemporary of Tertullian. Early on he was a practicing lawyer, but his conversion to Christianity led him to take on the position of full-time bishop in the church. It is said that he often deliberated on the freedom from sin he had come to know through his baptism. In *The Epistles of Cyprian*, notice Cyprian's allusion to Titus 3: 5 with the words "washing of regeneration," which he recognized as a depiction of baptism.

> But what a thing it is, to assert and contend that they who are not born in the Church can be the sons of God! For the blessed apostle sets forth and proves that baptism is that wherein the old man dies and the new man is born, saying, 'He saved us by the washing of regeneration.' But if regeneration is in the washing, that is, in baptism, how can heresy, which is not the spouse of Christ, generate sons to God by Christ?[65]

Many other Ante-Nicene Fathers wrote in complement with the ones noted here. These include men like Theophilus, Clement of Alexandria, Tatian the Syrian, Hippolytus, Origen, and others. In their writings they were unified in their awareness that baptism was regarded as the instrument designed by God whereby an individual, upon faith and repentance, receives forgiveness of sins and is spiritually regenerated. Rather than teaching that one is saved at the moment of belief in Jesus as God's Son, these men saw faith and repentance as indispensable requisites for baptism.

---

[63] Irenaeus, *Against Heresies*, bk. 1, chap. 21, sec. 1, http://www.earlychristianwritings.com/text/irenaeus-book1.html, accessed September 10, 2017.
[64] Tertullian, *On Baptism*, Early Christian Writings, http://www.earlychristianwritings.com/text/tertullian21.html accessed August 28, 2017.
[65] Cyprian, *The Epistles of Cyprian*, http://www.sacred-texts.com/chr/ecf/005/0050098.htm, accessed September 30, 2017.

Nicene and Post-Nicene Fathers

Aphrahat the Persian Sage (A.D. 280-345) lived during the time of the Nicene Council of the fourth century. His complement of works is titled *The Demonstrations*. He wrote the following powerful passage concerning the Spirit's involvement when one is baptized in Jesus' name.

> From baptism we receive the Spirit of Christ. At that same moment in which the priests invoke the Spirit, heaven opens, and he descends and rests upon the waters, and those who are baptized are clothed in him. The Spirit is absent from all those who are born of the flesh, until they come to the water of rebirth, and then they receive the Holy Spirit. . . . [I]n the second birth, that through baptism, they receive the Holy Spirit.[66]

Cyril of Jerusalem (A.D. 315-386), who served as a bishop in Jerusalem, was but a child during the Council of Nicea. He is on record as having participated in the acclaimed Council of Constantinople (A.D. 381). His writings on the subject of baptism are plentiful and substantive. Here are a few passages from his works.

> For all things whatsoever thou hast done shall be forgiven thee, whether it be fornication, or adultery, or any other such form of licentiousness. What can be greater sin than to crucify Christ? Yet even of this Baptism can purify. For so spake Peter to the three thousand who came to him, to those who had crucified the Lord, when they asked him, saying, 'Men and brethren, what shall we do?' For the wound is great. Thou hast made us think of our fall, O Peter, by saying, 'Ye killed the Prince of Life.' What salve is there for so great a wound? What cleansing for such foulness? What is the salvation for such perdition? 'Repent,' saith he, 'and be baptized every one of you in the name of Jesus Christ our Lord, for the remission of sins, and ye shall receive the gift of the Holy Ghost.' O unspeakable lovingkindness of God! They have no hope of being saved, and yet they are thought worthy of the Holy Ghost. Thou seest the power of Baptism! [67]

> The Lord... has granted repentance at Baptism, in order that we may cast off the chief - nay rather the whole burden of our sins, and having received the seal by the Holy Ghost, may be made heirs of eternal life.[68]

---

[66] Aphrahat, *The Demonstrations*, https://www.catholic.com/tract/baptismal-grace, accessed October 10, 2017
[67] Cyril of Jerusalem, 348AD, *"On Baptism,"* http://www.bebaptized.org/UndeniableFacts.htm, accessed October 12, 2017.
[68] Cyril of Jerusalem, 348AD, *"On Baptism,"* http://www.bebaptized.org/UndeniableFacts.htm, accessed October 12, 2017.

When going down, therefore, into the water, think not of the bare element, but look for salvation by the power of the Holy Ghost: for without both thou canst not possibly be made perfect. It is not I that say this, but the Lord Jesus Christ, who has the power in this matter: for He saith, 'Except a man be born anew' (and he adds the words) 'of water and of the Spirit, he cannot enter into the kingdom of God.' Neither doth he that is baptized with water, but not found worthy of the Spirit, receive the grace in perfection. Nor if a man be virtuous in his deeds, but receive not the seal by water, shall he enter into the kingdom of heaven.[69]

Basil of Caesarea (A.D. 329-379), also known as Saint Basil the Great, was born just a few years after the Council of Nicea. He was raised in a Christian home and learned the principles of Christianity from his family. His words concerning the role of baptism where salvation is concerned are insightful and inspiring.

Faith and baptism are two kindred and inseparable ways of salvation: faith is perfected through baptism, baptism is established through faith, and both are completed by the same names. For as we believe in the Father and the Son and the Holy Ghost, so are we also baptized in the name of the Father and of the Son and of the Holy Ghost; first comes the confession, introducing us to salvation, and baptism follows, setting the seal upon our assent.[70]

Gregory Nazianz (A.D. 325-389) was born in the year of the Council of Nicea. He was a close friend of Basil (above) and his father was bishop of Nazianzus at the time of his birth. In his work *Oration on Holy Baptism*, he noted:

Such is the grace and power of baptism; not an overwhelming of the world as of old, but a purification of the sins of each individual, and a complete cleansing from all the bruises and stains of sin. And since we are double-made, I mean of body and soul, and the one part is visible, the other invisible, so the cleansing also is twofold, by water and the spirit; the one received visibly in the body, the other concurring with it invisibly and apart from the body; the one typical, the other real and cleansing the depths.[71]

John Chrysostom (A.D. 347-407) was purportedly a very gifted speaker and has been called *the greatest preacher ever heard*. His

---

[69] Cyril of Jerusalem, *Catechetical Lectures*, http://www.bebaptized.org/UndeniableFacts.htm, accessed October 12, 2017.
[70] Basil the Great, *On the Holy Spirit*, Myriobiblos, http://www.myriobiblos.gr/texts/english/basil_spiritu_12.html, accessed September 5, 2017.
[71] Nazianz, Gregory, Oration on Holy Baptism https://biblehub.com/library/cyril/lectures_of_s_cyril_of_jerusalem/oration_xl_the_oration_on.htm, accessed October 10, 2017

articulation of doctrinal issues and godly principles was considered second to none by his peers. In *Homilies on Second Corinthians* he discussed the topic of baptism.

> In the Law, he that hath sin is punished; here, he that hath sins cometh and is baptized and is made righteous, and being made righteous, he liveth, being delivered from the death of sin... For in Baptism the sins are buried, the former things are blotted out, the man is made alive, the entire grace written upon his heart as it were a table.[72]

The Early Church Fathers had many disagreements and, where some doctrines are concerned, a number deviated substantially from the teachings of Scripture. Yet, it seems the one point that united them was their take on the significance and efficacy of baptism. They understood from the apostles that baptism is the moment of forgiveness of sins for the repentant believer. It is the God-appointed time when the Holy Spirit engages the human spirit and the believer begins participation in the kingdom. It is noteworthy that John 3: 3-5 was regarded by most of these men as a primary passage, and perhaps *the* primary passage, upon which this teaching is built. If Polycarp, a friend and student of the apostle who recorded Jesus' conversation with Nicodemus, understood that born of water means baptism, no one is in a position to question it two thousand years later.

The Pre-Reformation Perspective

Among early Reformation leaders, the name Martin Luther (1483-1546) stands out. It was Luther who developed and posted what is known as the Ninety-five Theses in 1517, charging the Roman Catholic Church with what he considered a form of *works salvation*. However, it is clear that baptism was not deemed a work by Luther and others in the early sixteenth century. On the contrary, he saw baptism as an instrument of God. His view on baptism was in line with that of the Apostolic and Early Church Fathers. Luther wrote:

> Baptism is no human plaything but is instituted by God himself. Moreover, it is solemnly and strictly commanded that we must be baptized or we shall not be saved. We are not to regard it as an indifferent matter, then, like putting

---

[72] Chrysostom, John, *Homilies on Second Corinthians*, 390 AD, https://biblehub.com/commentaries/chrysostom/2_corinthians/3.htm, accessed October 17, 2017.

on a new red coat. It is of the greatest importance that we regard baptism as excellent, glorious, and exalted.[73]

It is unsurprising that Luther viewed baptism as a salvific matter. This was the view of the church for more than fifteen centuries following Christ's ascension. Until the time of the Reformation Movement, the efficacy of baptism remained essentially unquestioned. The following is an excerpt from a published sermon of Luther. Here is what he had to say about Jesus' conversation with Nicodemus.

> 11. How a man is born anew may easily be told in words. When, however, it is a question of experience, as it was here with Nicodemus, then it is a hard matter to understand and it requires effort to attain the experience. It is easy to say: We must blind our reason, disregard our feelings, close our eyes and only cling to the Word--finally die and yet live. But to persevere in this, when it becomes a matter of experience and when we are really tested, requires pains and labor. It is a very bitter experience.
>
> 12. An example of this new birth we have in Abraham, whose son was to inherit the world and whose seed was to be like the stars in heaven, as was promised him in Gen 15:5. Then God came and commanded him to slay his son. Now had Abraham acted as reason dictated, he would have concluded thus: Aye, God has given me this seed, by which he has promised to increase my family, and now he commands me to offer him up as a sacrifice. Surely, God cannot command this; it must be the devil. But Abraham slays reason and honors God, thinking: God is so powerful that he can raise my son from death and increase my family through him. or he can give me another son, or effect his purpose in some other way, which I do not know. So Abraham commends all to God. Here Abraham leaves his old life and surrenders himself to God, believes in him and becomes a new man. Then the angel comes and says to him: "Abraham, Abraham, lay not thy hand upon the lad, neither do thou anything unto him: for now I know that thou fearest God, seeing thou hast not withheld thy son, thine only son, from me," Gen 22:11-12. Abraham could not have imagined that God would thus come to his rescue; nay, he had already in his heart slain his son.
>
> 13. Now, the beginning of this birth was in baptism. The water is baptism; the Spirit is that grace which is given to us in baptism. The result of this birth is clearly seen in the hour of death or in times of test by poverty and temptation. He who is born of the flesh fights to defend himself, looks hither and thither, employs his reason to make his living. But he who is born anew reasons thus: I am in God's hands, who has preserved and nourished me

---

[73] Luther, Martin. *The Necessity of Baptism*, http://www.catholic.com/tracts/the-necessity-of-baptism, accessed August 20, 2018.

before in a wonderful manner; he will also feed and preserve me in the future and save me from all sorrow and misfortune.[74]

Disederius Erasmus (1469-1536), an older contemporary of Luther and an early leader in the Reformation, disagreed with Luther on some doctrinal issues. However, where the efficacy of baptism was concerned, they held similar views. While the modern-day evangelical community rejects baptism as a matter of salvation, insisting that it equates to adding a human activity to the gospel message, Erasmus saw it a bit differently. Writing about Erasmus's perspective on the Great Commission, Darren T. Williamson wrote the following in his thesis of 2005.

> Erasmus concludes the section by assuring the newly baptized that their baptism was sufficient for salvation and there was no need to be 'burdened by Mosaic or human ceremonies,' which can add nothing to the simple and easily obtainable washing of baptism.[75]

The Post-Reformation Shift

The evangelical community has, over time, dramatically changed its stance on baptism. It has been designated a sign, a work, the new circumcision, and other labels not found in Scripture. However, even in the post-Reformation era, baptism was regarded as a matter of salvation by many church leaders. In the early seventeenth century, Thomas Helwys (1550-1616) and John Smyth (1570-1612) were involved as co-founders of what eventually became known as the Baptist denomination. Yet, in 1612, roughly four years prior to his death and ninety-five years after Luther posted his Ninety-five Theses on the door of the castle church in Wittenberg, Helwys wrote boldly and unambiguously not only concerning the rite of baptism, but specifically about Jesus' words in John 3: 5, stating:

> And our Savior Christ says, 'Except a man be born of water and of the Spirit, he cannot enter into the kingdom of God.' (John 3). And Hebrews 10:22, 'Let us draw near with a true heart in assurance of faith, our hearts being pure from evil confidence, and washed in our bodies with pure water.'

---

[74] Luther, Martin, *Martin Luther's Commentary*, https://www.stepbible.org/?q=version=Luther|reference=Joh.3, accessed August 19, 2018.
[75] Williamson, Darrel T., *Erasmus of Rotterdam's Influence upon Anabaptism: The Case of Belthasr Hubmaier*, Simon Frasier University, p 69.

Here is the true baptism set down, which is the baptism of amendment of life for the remission of sins. And here is the true matter where men must be washed, which is water and the Holy Ghost, that is pure from a evil conscience, and washed with water. Therefore can you not divide the water and the Spirit in this baptism. Christ has joined them together, and he that denies washing, or is not washed with the Spirit is not baptized, because we see the baptism of Christ is to be washed with water and the Holy Ghost."[76]

While Helwys and others stood firm in their view of the efficacy of baptism even beyond the Reformation Movement, many began to lean more heavily toward the teachings of Zwingli and Calvin. Eventually, the belief that baptism is unrelated to salvation began to dominate the Protestant landscape in the seventeenth and eighteenth centuries.

Many post-Reformation theologians have concluded that modern believers have been afforded a keener biblical perspective on baptism than were the Church Fathers. The argument is made that, with the fullness of canonized Scripture available, the modern-day church can better understand the teachings of the apostles to which these early believers were blind. Unlike these early Christians, modern scholars can better discern when Scripture does not say or mean what it says. It is now possible to see beyond the foolish teaching that baptism is a matter of spiritual consequence.

The claim that baptism is a sign that is unrelated to one's salvation might be taken seriously if but a few outliers in the early church taught of the efficacy of baptism. Yet, this truth permeated church teaching at all levels for fifteen hundred years. Therefore, it cannot be dismissed as a naive misreading of apostolic instruction by a few. The Church Fathers considered the redemptive worth of baptism to be at the very heart of the apostles' teaching.

The modern view of baptism clashes dramatically with that of the Church Fathers. The problem for evangelical theologians who see baptism differently than the Church Fathers is that, in order to secure biblical support for this modern-day view, each passage of Scripture that teaches of the redemptive role of baptism (and there are many) must be recast to say something it does not say. This was not a problem for the Church Fathers since, for them, Scripture simply meant what it said concerning the efficacy of baptism.

---

[76] Helwys, Thomas, & Richard Groves (Ed.). (1998.) *The Mystery of Iniquity Book 1*, Mercer University Press. 1998, p.103.

Chapter 8
Baptism and Regeneration

Regeneration

A number of words and phrases in Scripture hold salvific significance. For instance, forgiveness of sins is often presented in connection with salvation. As discussed earlier, Paul recognized a direct relationship between forgiveness and redemption in some of his epistles (Ephesians 1: 7; Colossians 1: 13-14). Consequently, when forgiveness of sins is addressed in Scripture (cf. Acts 10: 43; 26: 18), it is a forgiveness that comes from God and affords the recipient of that forgiveness redemption through Christ's blood. Sins must be forgiven for one to be saved.

When Jesus was on earth, he claimed the authority to forgive sins even though his blood had not yet been shed. This explains why he was able to forgive a paralytic man (Matthew 9: 2-6) as well as the thief who died on the cross next to him (Luke 23: 39-43). (Scripture does not specifically state that Jesus forgave the thief of his sins, but this can be inferred since he promised to take the thief with him to Paradise).

The term *born again* also speaks to redemption/salvation. John and Peter were known for using this expression on occasion (John 3: 3, 7; 1 Peter 1: 3, 23). Each time they wrote or spoke these words they had man's eternal salvation in view. Other expressions also reflect the idea of being born again. These include phrases like "born of God" (John 1: 13; 1 John 3: 9) "being renewed" (2 Corinthians 4: 16, Colossians 3: 10), and "newness of life" (Romans 6: 4).

One word that has caught the attention of many and speaks to the idea of being born again is the term "regeneration" (Titus 3: 5). In physical birth a life is generated (thus the term 'generations'). When one is regenerated (spiritually) he/she takes on a new spiritual identity that is provided through the work of the Holy Spirit and by the blood of Christ as sins are washed away and a new, pure life emerges.

Baptismal Regeneration

One expression that has been bandied about recently is *baptismal regeneration*. What is baptismal regeneration? The expression holds different meanings for different people. Some (e.g., the Roman Catholic Church) believe baptism is a religious sacrament. The idea of a sacrament is that an activity or ceremony holds an innate capacity to effect change. For instance, the sacramental view of baptism is that the baptismal water has been empowered in some mystical sense (viz., holy water) to remove sins. Consequently, even someone with no faith (e.g., an infant) may be cleansed of sin and attain salvation through the intrinsic power of baptism.

The Bible does not teach baptismal regeneration, at least not in a sacramental sense. That is not to say that baptism is unrelated to one's salvation. According to Scripture, baptism is the biblically appointed time when God has promised to respond, providing regeneration for the believing repentant who humbly submits to baptism in Jesus' name. This is not sacramental baptism as many have asserted. Biblical submission to baptism is one's appeal to God in Jesus' name (1 Peter 3: 21), per his instructions, for forgiveness of sins (Acts 2: 38) and the opportunity to experience newness of life (Romans 6: 1-4). God responds in kind, removing one's sinful self (Colossians 2: 11) and replacing it, spiritually speaking, with a new, forgiven creature.

Baptism is a redemptive matter, but many who teach this do not generally think in terms of baptismal regeneration because they do not think in terms of sacraments. However, the evangelical community not only denies the biblically prescribed link between baptism and forgiveness/salvation, but they seem to look down on any who respect that connection. Consequently, the expression *baptismal regeneration* is often employed furtively by evangelicals as a pejorative aimed at those who teach that baptism does, in fact, have a place in the biblical plan of salvation. The intent is to subtly lay at the feet of such a one the charge of teaching *another gospel* against which Paul warned the early church (Galatians 1: 8).

The Bible portrays baptism as an ordinance that, when accompanied by one's repentance and faith in the redemptive power of Jesus' death and resurrection, results in forgiveness of sins and the bestowal of eternal life. Baptism does not have innate spiritual power, but it is the time appointed by God for one's transition from spiritual death to spiritual life. The ceremony itself was designed by God to commemorate the death, burial, and resurrection of Jesus. Through submission to baptism, as a matter of faithful response to godly instruction, the individual honors Jesus' sacrifice.

Baptism and the Spirit

What is the relationship between baptism and the Holy Spirit? The biblical answer to this question coincidently provides insight into what occurs during one's submission to baptism in Jesus' name. It also explains why Jesus told Nicodemus that one must be born of water and the Spirit in order to enter the kingdom of heaven.

God's Word teaches that people are cleansed/saved by the blood of Christ. The very purpose of his sacrifice was that each one might be forgiven of sins and reconciled to God (Matthew 26: 28; Acts 20: 28; Romans 3: 25; Ephesians 1: 7; Colossians 1: 20; Hebrews 9: 12-14; 1 Peter 1: 18-19; 1 John 1: 7). This is a message that permeates the pages of Scripture.

The knowledge that salvation is available only through the blood of Christ gives rise to a couple of thoughts. First, understanding *how* this spiritual cleansing takes place seems worthy of consideration. Also, and equally important, deliberation should be given to *when* one is cleansed by his blood according to Scripture. If it is unknown *when* this cleansing occurs, it is not possible to know *if* it has happened.

Men have sinned against God (Romans 3: 23). Each one who is guilty of sin has, by the very nature of the act, incurred a debt that is owed to God. Paul explained this to the church in Colosse when writing about forgiveness of sins and the rationale for Jesus' sacrifice.

[9] For in Him all the fullness of Deity dwells in bodily form, [10] and in Him you have been made complete, and He is the head over all rule and authority; [11] and in Him you were also circumcised with a circumcision made without hands, in the removal of the body of the flesh by the circumcision of Christ; [12] having been buried with Him in baptism, in which you were also raised up with Him through faith in the working of God, who raised Him from the dead. [13] When you were dead in your transgressions and the uncircumcision of your flesh, He made you alive together with Him, having forgiven us all our

transgressions, [14] **having canceled out the certificate of debt** consisting of decrees against us, which was hostile to us; and He has taken it out of the way, having nailed it to the cross." (Colossians 2: 9-14) – emphasis added

In what sense does sin result in debt? There are a couple of ways to look at this. First of all, though people have freedom through Christ (Acts 13: 39), that freedom is accessible only because Jesus has paid the price for the sins of humanity (Galatians 5: 1). God has established natural moral laws that are to be obeyed. Just as those who break human laws must face the consequences of their actions, so those who break God's laws are held accountable.

Another way to understand man's debt to God is that he has created humankind for a specific purpose. Paul, in writing to the church in Ephesus, told the believers there:

> For we are His workmanship, created in Christ Jesus for good works, which God prepared beforehand so that we would walk in them. (Ephesians 2: 10)

God created mankind "…for good works." In much the same way that someone might hire another to fulfill a task, God has given humanity life that they might do good works in accord with godliness. If a person has been paid to accomplish something and they do not, they would naturally owe the person who hired them for their lack of service. In that same vein, when people fail to accomplish that for which they were given life, by nature they owe God for the life he has given them. That is why "…the wages of sin is death" (Romans 6: 23) – the forfeiture of life is payment for sins committed.

God is holy and does not commune with that which is unholy (Habakkuk 1: 13). Yet, sin makes men unholy. For one to become holy, the person's sins must be removed. The forfeiture of life – payment for the cost of sins – was paid by Jesus. Living a perfect, sinless life, Jesus was the only one in a position to pay that price for all who have sinned. His blood, then, is the only cleansing agent by which sins might be removed and communion with God restored.

While Christ's blood is the cleansing agent by which sins are remitted, this sanctifying work is accomplished through the work of the Holy Spirit, which was discussed in chapter 5. It is through the regeneration provided by the Spirit that one is spiritually renewed. This is what John the Baptist had in view when he stated:

> [7]...After me One is coming who is mightier than I, and I am not fit to stoop down and untie the thong of His sandals. [8] I baptized you with water; but He will baptize you with the Holy Spirit. (Mark 1: 7-8)

This prophecy by John, which was discussed earlier, represents the initial recognition of the coming connection between baptism and the Holy Spirit. It is a relationship that would not be fully realized until the Day of Pentecost. On that day, Peter told the crowd in Jerusalem:

> Repent, and each of you be baptized in the name of Jesus Christ for the forgiveness of your sins; and you will receive the gift of the Holy Spirit. (Acts 2: 38)

The Spirit's dual role with respect to conversion is explored openly in God's Word. On the Day of Pentecost, Peter was speaking of the indwelling presence of the Holy Spirit that is promised to obedient believers (Romans 8: 9; 1 Corinthians 6: 19; 2 Corinthians 1: 22). However, other New Testament passages explain the Spirit's role in the regenerating process that occurs during baptism.

> Such were some of you; but you were washed, but you were sanctified, but you were justified in the name of the Lord Jesus Christ and in the Spirit of our God. (1 Corinthians 6: 11)

> He saved us, not on the basis of deeds which we have done in righteousness, but according to His mercy, by the washing of regeneration and renewing by the Holy Spirit. (Titus 3: 5)

> [1] Peter, an apostle of Jesus Christ,
> To those who reside as aliens, scattered throughout Pontus, Galatia, Cappadocia, Asia, and Bithynia, who are chosen [2] according to the foreknowledge of God the Father, by the sanctifying work of the Spirit, to obey Jesus Christ and be sprinkled with His blood: May grace and peace be yours in the fullest measure. (1 Peter 1: 1-2)

Many people maintain that only belief in Jesus as Savior is necessary for one to receive forgiveness and salvation, but that is not the lesson of God's Word. The lesson from Scripture is that God equates belief and obedience. That is to say, if one has not obeyed the fullness of the gospel message, one has not believed.

> He who believes in the Son has eternal life; but he who does not obey the Son will not see life, but the wrath of God abides on him. (John 3: 36)

> And we are witnesses of these things; and *so is* the Holy Spirit, whom God has given to those who obey Him. (Acts 5: 32)
>
> ...dealing out retribution to those who do not know God and to those who do not obey the gospel of our Lord Jesus. (2 Thessalonians 1: 8)
>
> And having been made perfect, He became to all those who obey Him the source of eternal salvation. (Hebrews 5: 9)
>
> For *it is* time for judgment to begin with the household of God; and if *it begins* with us first, what *will be* the outcome for those who do not obey the gospel of God? (1 Peter 4: 17)

According to Scripture, one's sins are forgiven and the Holy Spirit is received upon repentance of sins and baptism in Jesus' name (Acts 2: 38). This explains the emphasis on obedience in these verses. The Spirit is given, not to those who believe (although belief is necessary), but to those who obey. Jesus is the source of eternal salvation to those who obey Him. Additionally, purification of one's soul is accomplished, not when one believes, but when he/she obeys.

Change of State

Obedience to the gospel message is not a matter of simply having a changed mind or a changed heart. It is about experiencing a change of state. The New Testament emphasizes that a change of state (from dead in sin to alive in Christ) takes place when one is obedient in baptism and that, absent that obedience, no change of state occurs. Alexander Campbell (1788-1866) wrote concerning this change:

> ...no change of heart is equivalent to or can be substituted for a change of state!"[77]

Campbell continued, drilling down on what is necessary for one to experience a changed state. Looking to the Great Commission, he noted the following concerning Jesus' words.

> The commission of converting the world teaches that immersion was necessary to discipleship; for Jesus said, "Convert the nations, immersing them into the name," etc., and "teaching them to observe," etc. The construction of the sentence fairly indicates that no person can be a disciple, according to the commission, who has not been immersed; *for the active*

---

[77] Campbell, Alexander, *The Christian System*, Gospel Advocate Company, Nashville, TN, 2001, p. 163.

participle in connection with an imperative either declares the manner in which the imperative shall be obeyed, or explains the meaning of the command.

To this I have found no exception. For example: - "Cleanse the house, sweeping it"; "Cleanse the garment, washing it," shows the manner in which the command is to be obeyed, or explains the meaning of it. Thus, "Convert [or disciple] the nations, immersing them and teaching them to observe," etc., expresses the manner in which the command is to be obeyed.[78]

Salvation is not available through disobedient faith. Indeed, disobedient faith is not the faith of the Bible (James 2: 24). According to Paul, those who fail to obey the gospel will receive retribution.

...dealing out retribution to those who do not know God and to those who do not obey the gospel of our Lord Jesus. (2 Thessalonians 1: 8).

These two ideas – not knowing God and not obeying the gospel – are joined by the conjunction *kai* that, by coincidence, is the same conjunction Jesus used in John 3: 5 where it joins born of water *and* (kai) the Spirit. Here Paul uses the word to conjoin two classes of people who will experience the same eternal consequence. Coffman states concerning the Thessalonians passage:

Implicit...in the adverse judgment to be pronounced against them that "know not God," is the fact of their "refusing to know God" (Romans 1:20-28) and of their being in no sense innocent, but "without excuse." In the second class, it...refers with equal power to "unbelievers" of all races and nations, even professing Christians, who refuse to "obey the gospel." And what does that mean? It means those who refuse to be baptized into Christ and to assume the duties and obligations incumbent upon all true Christians.[79]

Obedience to the faith is an expression occasionally used by the New Testament writers (cf. Acts 6: 7; Romans 1: 5; 16: 26). It is one thing to have faith. However, according to Scripture, it is a separate matter to be obedient to the faith. It is not by faith, but through an obedient act resulting from faith wherein a person experiences a change of state. That change of state occurs during baptism.

---

[78] Campbell, Alexander, *The Christian System*, Gospel Advocate Company, Nashville, TN, 2001, p. 170.
[79] Coffman, James B., *James Burton Coffman Commentaries: 1&2 Thessalonians, 1&2 Timothy, Titus, and Philemon*, ACU Press, Abilene, TX, 1986, p. 86.

An individual is baptized for forgiveness of sins (Acts 2: 38). Cleansing comes through the washing with water in order that one might be presented to Christ without spot or wrinkle (Ephesians 5: 26). Salvation comes through the bath of regeneration and the renewing work of the Holy Spirit (Titus 3: 5).

These verses spell out at least one element of what the apostles meant when they spoke of obedience. Scripture portrays baptism as the God-ordained moment when one's sins are forgiven and the individual is regenerated as a new creature in Christ. In baptism a person experiences the change of state necessary to be a child of God. Paul wrote to the Galatians concerning this change of state.

> "[23] But before faith came, we were kept in custody under the law, being shut up to the faith which was later to be revealed. [24] Therefore the Law has become our tutor *to lead us* to Christ, so that we may be justified by faith. [25] But now that faith has come, we are no longer under a tutor. [26] For you are all sons of God through faith in Christ Jesus. [27] For all of you who were baptized into Christ have clothed yourselves with Christ." (Galatians 3: 23-27)

Paul places considerable emphasis on baptism in this passage even though it is faith that is recognized as the means of justification. While men attempt to isolate baptism from faith, Paul does not. Instead, he thoughtfully connects them. Baptism is fundamental, according to Paul, even in the presence of faith. Prior to faith men were kept under tutorship by the law. However, baptism is presented as an explanation of how/when people are saved by faith.

Paul describes baptism as a passageway through which a person could find his/her way into Christ. He points out that *putting on* Christ is limited to "...all of you who were baptized" (v. 27). In a message that focuses on faith, Paul is firm in his presentation of baptism as a step *into* Christ. This is in keeping with Jesus' words to Nicodemus when he said, "...unless one is born of water and the Spirit" (John 3: 5).

Having explained to the Galatians that they had been justified by faith (vv. 23-26), Paul begins verse 27 with a curious word. It is the word *for*, translated from the Greek word *gar*. According to *Strong's Exhaustive Concordance of the Bible* this word *assigns a reason* to the statement(s) made. Consider the intricate design of his remarks:

> But before faith came, we were kept in custody under the law...Therefore the Law has become our tutor *to lead us* to Christ...But now that faith has come, we are no longer under a tutor. For (the reason is) you are all sons of God

through faith in Christ Jesus. For (the reason is) all of you who were baptized into Christ have clothed yourselves with Christ. (Galatians 3: 23-27)

The apostle's point is clear when his words are given honest consideration. The bond he establishes between baptism and a person's change of state (from spiritual death to a regenerated spiritual life) is unmistakable. The reason one can claim justification by faith (v. 24) and graduation from the state of tutorship (v. 25) is that he has become a son of God through faith (v. 26). The reason he is deemed to be a son of God through faith is that, having been baptized into Christ, he has put on Christ (v. 27). Jack Cottrell wrote concerning this verse:

>...faith and baptism are related to sonship. They are specified here as two basic conditions for becoming one with Christ and thus sons and heirs with Him.[80]

One's spiritual change of state is what Paul has in view in the Galatians passage. While faith plays an indispensable role in that transformation, according to the apostle it is neither the single nor the final determinant of that change. Spiritual transformation (change of state) occurs when a believer, as a matter of faith in Jesus' death, burial, and resurrection, repents of his sins and submits to baptism in Jesus' name where he is cleansed by the blood of Christ and regenerated by the Spirit.

Sinners have no standing before God to seek forgiveness. The cost of sin can be satisfied only through blood sacrifice (Hebrews 9: 22). It is repentance and submission to baptism in Jesus' name (invoking the efficacy of his sacrifice) that positions the sinner for forgiveness during baptism. God has promised that the repentant sinner will rise from the water in a changed state, having received "newness of life" (Romans 6: 4). It is a person's faith in that promise to which he gracefully responds. The lost soul receives redemption – forgiveness of sins – by God's grace, through faith, upon obedience in baptism.

---

[80] Cottrell, Jack, *Baptism A Biblical Study*, College Press Publishing, Jopplin, MO, 1989, p. 106.

Chapter 9

Baptism as a Sign of Salvation

Searching Scripture

It is fascinating to note how many commonly used expressions are deemed to have biblical origin when such is not the case. For instance, many believe that the phrase *cleanliness is next to godliness* is drawn directly from Scripture. Yet, these words in this form do not appear in God's Word. While both the Old and New Testaments speak at length of cleanliness and purity, the focus is generally on spiritual purity. Less attention is given to physical cleanliness, though ceremonial washings were incorporated into the Israelites' worship of God.

The same is true of other expressions. As an example, many like to use the phrase *God helps those who help themselves*. Certainly, the principle of working hard is biblical and prime examples can be found in Scripture. Noah evidently worked for decades building an ark per God's instructions (Genesis 6: 1-22) and Jacob labored fourteen years to win Rachel as his bride (Genesis 29: 18-28). While the principle that God respects those who work hard can be easily drawn from Scripture, the expression *God helps those who help themselves* cannot be found in the Bible.

It may come as a surprise to many, but the phrase *God works in mysterious ways* cannot be found in God's Word. That is not to say that Scripture is not filled with instances where God works mysteriously. Holy Writ holds example after example of God providing, revealing, and working in ways that are well beyond human understanding (cf. Isaiah 55: 8; Daniel 2: 19; 1 Timothy 3: 16). The Apostle Paul even described faith itself as a mystery (1 Timothy 3: 9). Certainly, then, God does work in mysterious ways, but the expression itself originated outside of God's Word.

These are three common examples of idioms that people wrongfully attribute to Scripture and there are many more. There is nothing wrong with providing a clean environment, working hard, and respecting the mysteries of God. The fact that these are not biblical expressions does not mean they are harmful or lacking in wisdom. In truth, respecting these principles may well improve the conditions of one's life.

Baptism as a Sign

Two common expressions with respect to baptism have been repeated continuously over the past few hundred years. In fact, they have been used time and again by those who profess biblical scholarship. Because they are embraced so casually as elementary biblical principles by those who claim expert biblical knowledge, they have become accepted by many as a true characterization of the rite of baptism as it is taught in God's Word.

The first saying that has developed into a seemingly household expression over the years is the claim that *baptism is a sign of salvation*. This statement has given birth to the second, which is that baptism is *an outward sign of an inward grace*. It is critical to note that neither of these statements can be found in Scripture. The truth is, neither of these *teachings* can be found there. It is granted that baptism, a physical act, is visible to the human eye, but that does not make it a sign.

While men like Zwingli and Calvin may have laid the groundwork, those who followed after them eventually pared down the concept of saving faith to a personal acknowledgement that Jesus is Lord and that he died for the sins of men. It is taught that this belief/acknowledgement alone results in salvation. Focused on the principle that salvation is "...not as a result of works" (Ephesians 2: 9), it was determined by subsequent generations that human *activity* in obeying the gospel message must constitute work (salvation by merit). As such, any teaching that involves human activity in response to the gospel message as a matter of salvation (e.g., baptism) must be rejected as unbiblical. Therefore, it was decided that baptism must be considered a sign of salvation.

Baptism and Circumcision

John Calvin, who struggled mightily with Scripture's portrayal of baptism as a matter of salvation, chose to reject it. He finally settled in his own mind that baptism, like circumcision in the Old Testament, was intended as a sign of covenant participation. According to Calvin, where the relationship between circumcision and baptism was concerned:

> ...there is no difference in the internal meaning, from which the whole power and peculiar nature of the sacrament is to be estimated. The only difference which remains is in the external ceremony.[81]

Calvin drew his claim that baptism was the new covenant circumcision from Paul's reference to circumcision in his letter to the Colossians. In that letter Paul likened the removal of one's sins during baptism to the removal of the male infant's foreskin in circumcision (Colossians 2: 11-12). It was this connection, along with his rejection of any link between baptism and redemption, that led Calvin to his conclusion. Here is the specific passage Calvin used to make this determination.

> [11] and in Him you were also circumcised with a circumcision made without hands, in the removal of the body of the flesh by the circumcision of Christ; [12] having been buried with Him in baptism, in which you were also raised up with Him through faith in the working of God, who raised Him from the dead. [13] When you were dead in your transgressions and the uncircumcision of your flesh, He made you alive together with Him, having forgiven us all our transgressions, [14] having canceled out the certificate of debt consisting of decrees against us, which was hostile to us; and He has taken it out of the way, having nailed it to the cross. (Colossians 2: 11-14)

There are some important things to consider about this passage. Calvin believed Paul was describing baptism as a manner of New Testament circumcision, but that is not what Paul wrote. Circumcision is not likened to baptism in these verses. It is "...the removal of the body of flesh" (removal of sins) that is characterized as a type of circumcision. Paul used an analogy – a figure of speech – to describe for his readers what occurs during baptism.

The weakness of Calvin's position is demonstrated in an incident that took place during the early stages of the church (Acts 15: 1-11) Certain Jews from the church in Antioch argued with the Apostle Paul, insisting that Gentiles must become circumcised to participate in the kingdom of heaven. They were essentially saying that a Gentile must convert to Judaism prior to becoming a Christian. To settle this

---

[81] Calvin, John, *Institutes of the Christian Religion*, Hendrickson Publishers, Book Fourth, Peabody, MA, 2008,, p. 874.

argument, Paul and others traveled to Jerusalem where the apostles could address the question. The apostles and elders in Jerusalem determined that, in fact, circumcision was not necessary for Gentiles in the church age.

What is most significant in this episode, particularly given Calvin's assertion, is that the subject of baptism never surfaced. If baptism was meant to replace circumcision and the apostles were aware of this, they would have said so at this time since it was their responsibility to teach the full truth of God. Their silence concerning any connection between the two at the time of the Jerusalem Council fully repudiates Calvin's position.

Rather than teaching baptism as the new circumcision, "The apostles and the elders came together to look into this matter" (Acts 15: 6). Thus, they considered the necessity of circumcision even in the presence of baptism. Furthermore, Christian Jews practiced circumcision faithfully after the Jerusalem Council even as they submitted to Christ in baptism. Consequently, the early church was comprised of both circumcised and uncircumcised believers. It is evident, then, that a relationship between Christian baptism and the circumcision of Israelite infants was never contemplated in the first century church. Circumcision served as a sign of the Abrahamic covenant while baptism serves as a doorway to the kingdom of heaven through the remission of sins.

Defining a Covenant Sign

A covenant sign is a symbol that represents the covenant with all its promises and expectations. This is what differentiates baptism and circumcision. God declared circumcision to be the sign of his covenant with Abraham (Genesis 17: 11) just as the rainbow was designated as a sign of God's covenant with Noah (Genesis 9: 13).

Biblically speaking, how does one determine whether something like baptism or circumcision is a covenant sign? A covenant sign must exhibit certain characteristics. First and foremost, its status as a covenant sign must be a matter of declaration rather than speculation. In addressing this requirement, Arnold G. Fruchtenbaum, an expert in the Old Testament and Hebrew culture, remarked:

> …what is a sign of a covenant is what God calls a sign of a covenant and therefore, I would agree that 'a sign must be formally declared.'[82]

---

[82] This quote was received in a personal e-mail from Mr. Frutchenbaum to the author of this book.

God established a number of covenants with men in the Old Testament including his covenant with Moses (Exodus 34: 27) and the covenant he established with David through the prophet Nathan (2 Samuel 7: 4-17). Interestingly, no covenant sign is named in the Davidic covenant. This is not remarkable, though. According to Fruchtenbaum:

> Not every covenant came with a sign or token.[83]

The history of covenant signs in Scripture reveals one additional common trait. A consistent feature of a covenant sign, such as the Sabbath Day (Exodus 31: 13-17) or the rainbow (Genesis 9: 11-17), is that it *persists* throughout the life of the covenant, either perpetually (circumcision) or repeatedly (rainbow), as a reminder of promises made within the framework of the covenant. Since the purpose of a covenant sign is remembrance, its continuation is critical. It stands to reason that this is why God established circumcision rather than childbirth as the Abrahamic covenant sign. Childbirth occurs only once and served as the means of entrance into that covenant. Circumcision served as a perpetual reminder of the covenant through the life of Abraham's descendants.

Finally, a covenant sign generally involves some kind of pledge between the parties involved. For Abraham, the pledge was God's promises concerning his descendants (Genesis 17: 15-16). With the rainbow, God promised Noah that he would never again destroy mankind with a flood (Genesis 9: 11-17).

When it comes to biblical covenants, the words *sign* and *seal* seem to be applied interchangeably. For instance, Paul wrote concerning Abraham:

> ...and he received the sign of circumcision, a seal of the righteousness of the faith which he had while uncircumcised, so that he might be the father of all who believe without being circumcised, that righteousness might be credited to them. (Romans 4: 11)

Has a sign been established for the covenant of grace? There are two elements of the covenant that seem to fit the continuation and remembrance criteria of a sign. Numerous times in the New Testament mention is made that those who are in Christ have been sealed by the

---

[83] Frutchenbaum, Arnold G., *The Eight Covenants of the Bible* http://www.messianicassociation.org/ezine17-af.covenants.htm, accessed January 20, 2018.

Holy Spirit (2 Corinthians 1: 22; Ephesians 1: 13; 4: 30). Also, the Lord's Supper seems to fit the bill on both counts.

If a covenant sign and seal can be equated, and this seems to be a reasonable conclusion grounded in Scripture, the gift of the Holy Spirit that believers receive has been declared and serves as a sign of the covenant. Similarly, Jesus introduced the Lord's Supper to his disciples as both a matter of repetition and remembrance (1 Corinthians 11: 23-26). Still, Jesus did not declare the Lord's Supper as a sign or seal. Instead, it is presented as an ordinance established by God. In that sense, it more closely resembles the rites performed by the priests of the first covenant than a sign.

While Jesus told Nicodemus that a man must be reborn (spiritually), this spiritual rebirth is not deemed a sign of the covenant any more than childbirth was considered a sign of the Abrahamic covenant. Those who insist that baptism is a covenant sign have eclipsed what Scripture has to offer. Others may argue that, even if baptism is not a covenant sign, *per se*, it might still be considered a sign, or token of salvation that has already taken place. Is this the case?

Few would challenge the ingenuity of Charles Spurgeon (1834-1892). He was a Baptist evangelist and writer whose pen and wit were as sharp as any. Even those who might differ with him theologically recognize his innovative manner of teaching.

As a Baptist preacher, Spurgeon was opposed to the concept of infant baptism. Baptist doctrine states that baptism is intended for those who believe that Jesus is God's Son and that it is by immersion only. Since infants cannot believe in Jesus and are sprinkled rather than immersed, Spurgeon considered them unqualified as candidates for baptism. The idea is not that infants are unworthy, but that the sprinkling of water serves no purpose where infants are concerned. He constantly challenged those who practiced infant baptism, insisting that it was an unbiblical practice. In that vein, he cleverly wrote the following.

> If we could find infant baptism in the word of God, we should adopt it. It would help us out of a great difficulty, for it would take away from us that reproach which is attached to us, that we are odd, and do not as other people do. But we have looked well through the Bible, and cannot find it, and do not believe that it is there; nor do we believe that others can find infant baptism in the Scriptures, unless they themselves first put it there.[84]

---

[84] Spurgeon, Charles Haddon, Spurgeon, Susannah, Harrald, Joseph, *The Autobiography of Charles H. Spurgeon*, Vol. 1, Chicago: F.H. Revell, 1898, p. 155.

This represents a cunning method for challenging those with whom one might doctrinally disagree. Perhaps, then, this same approach could be used to consider certain other doctrines that seem to lack biblical support. For instance, suppose the words *infant baptism* were replaced with, say, *baptism is a sign of salvation*. It stands to reason that if this phrase could be found in Scripture, the principle should be adopted. This would be helpful in that, "…it would take away from us that reproach which is attached to us, that we are odd, and do not as other people do." However, as with infant baptism, the teaching that baptism is a sign of salvation cannot be found in God's Word. It must be the case, then, that modern men "…first put it there." The same would be true of the expression *baptism is an outward sign of an inward grace*. Similarly, *The Sinner's Prayer* could be effectively substituted for infant baptism in Spurgeon's challenge with the same result.

The teaching that baptism is a sign of salvation and has no connection to forgiveness has dominated evangelical doctrine since the Reformation Movement of the sixteenth century. It is said that those passages of Scripture that present baptism as a matter of redemption are either poorly written or the true meaning has been lost in translation. A tangled set of syntactical gymnastics is then offered to explain why these verses do not mean or say what they state plainly. It is a curious matter that it is primarily baptism-related texts that must be corrected by modern men. For those who question this approach to understanding Scripture, perhaps those passages that speak of the spiritual change that occurs during baptism deserve a second, and even a third look.

Chapter 10

Baptism and Necessity

Born of Water

With the words *born of water*, Jesus was speaking to Nicodemus about baptism (immersion in water). Yet, it is probably more accurate to say that the entire phrase *born of water and the Spirit* is intended to depict baptism as Jesus recognized the spiritual transformation through the work of the Holy Spirit that occurs at that time. Jesus' words were intended to complement his Great Commission, presented below by Matthew and Mark respectively, where he instructed the disciples to teach and baptize the nations.

> [19] Go therefore and make disciples of all the nations, baptizing them in the name of the Father and the Son and the Holy Spirit, [20] teaching them to observe all that I commanded you; and lo, I am with you always, even to the end of the age. (Matthew 28: 19-20)

> [15] And He said to them, 'Go into all the world and preach the gospel to all creation. [16] He who has believed and has been baptized shall be saved; but he who has disbelieved shall be condemned.' (Mark 16: 15-16)

Jesus made two distinct statements in Mark 16: 16. In the first portion of the verse (16a) Jesus stated, "He who has believed and has been baptized shall be saved." In the next portion (16b) he finished his teaching, stating, "...he who has disbelieved shall be condemned."

Modern scholarship has gone to great lengths to neutralize the teaching found in 16a where, without ambiguity, Jesus identified the saved as those who believe and receive baptism. It is said that because, in 16b, Jesus proclaimed condemnation only for unbelievers, he arguably left the door open to the teaching that baptism is not necessarily a condition for salvation and that only those who do not believe are condemned. The un-immersed, it is said, are not automatically disqualified from salvation. Yet, Jesus told the disciples, "He who has believed and has been baptized shall be saved." With these words, the saved are identified as baptized believers. Nothing more is necessary to understand that truth.

Jesus wanted to provide the disciples with the full picture of judgment. The saved status of baptized believers says nothing about the eternal fortune of unbelievers. What does their future hold? According to Jesus, they are condemned. It would have been the ultimate redundancy for Jesus to comment on the condemnation of the un-immersed since unbelievers are by default un-immersed. The claim that the un-immersed might be saved flatly contradicts Jesus' words in 16a.

Jesus was not, with the statement "...he who has disbelieved shall be condemned," negating what he had just said concerning salvation. There is no change in the terms of salvation between 16a and 16b. It is baptized believers who will be saved, and Jesus has stated this in no uncertain terms. Jesus' words in Mark 16 complement the many passages of Scripture where baptism is presented, either through teaching or conversion examples, as a matter of regeneration, forgiveness, salvation, and newness of life.

The Early Church Fathers were clear in their teaching concerning baptism. In a passage mentioned a bit earlier, Justin Martyr identified the un-immersed as unbelievers. In a statement that directly complements Jesus' words in Mark 16: 16, he wrote:

> ...the one who refuses to be baptized is to be condemned as an unbeliever, partially on the basis of what Jesus told Nicodemus....'He that, out of contempt, will not be baptized, shall be condemned as an unbeliever, and shall be reproached as ungrateful and foolish.' [85]

Absolute Necessity

It is difficult to escape the firmness with which Jesus impressed upon Nicodemus the terms for seeing (participating in) the kingdom of God. One cannot read Jesus' words "...unless one is born again" and subscribe to a view that one can see the kingdom without being reborn.

---

[85] Martyr, Justin, *Constitutions of the Holy Apostles*, www.bebaptized.org/UndeniableFacts.htm, accessed October 25, 2017.

The Greek *ean me* speaks specifically to limited options, much like its English counterpart *unless*, as seen in the following verses.

> For I say to you that unless (ean me) your righteousness surpasses *that* of the scribes and Pharisees, you will not enter the kingdom of heaven. (Matthew 5: 20)
>
> Truly I say to you, unless (ean me) you are converted and become like children, you will not enter the kingdom of heaven. (Matthew 18: 3)
>
> He went away again a second time and prayed, saying, 'My Father, if this cannot pass away unless (ean me) I drink it, Your will be done.' (Matthew 26: 42)
>
> I tell you, no, but unless (ean me) you repent, you will all likewise perish. (Luke 13: 3)
>
> Therefore I said to you that you will die in your sins; for unless (ean me) you believe that I am *He*, you will die in your sins. (John 8: 24)

Each of these verses speaks to a person's salvation in some sense. For instance, one cannot anticipate salvation with righteousness that fails to surpass that of the scribes and Pharisees (Matthew 5: 20). Also, a person must be converted and become like a child to become a part of God's kingdom (Matthew 18: 3). Jesus was required to drink the cup of sacrifice so that mankind might be saved (Matthew 26: 42). Both repentance and belief are essential for one to know salvation (Luke 13: 3; John 8: 24). In similar fashion, Jesus told Nicodemus, "...unless one is born again he cannot see the kingdom of God" (John 3: 3). Consequently, like belief and repentance, rebirth is not an option, but a requisite for seeing the kingdom.

Nicodemus's own words early in the conversation provide a sense of the limited options provided with *ean me*. Approaching Jesus, he stated, "Rabbi, we know that You have come from God *as* a teacher; for no one can do these signs that You do unless (ean me) God is with him" (John 3: 2). In other words, at least from Nicodemus's perspective, the *only* way Jesus could do the things he had done was through the power of God. The expression carries this same force in Jesus' words. The only way to participate in the kingdom of heaven is to be born of water and the Spirit.

In his words to Nicodemus, Jesus portrayed baptism as a condition for entering the kingdom. Given the straightforward character of his words, one might even argue that he made it an unqualified condition. How, then, can men consider baptism anything but the single moment, biblically speaking, when one connects with the Holy Spirit and Christ's blood and is born again?

Like belief and repentance, immersion in water must not be overlooked by those who seek to be a part of the kingdom and attain salvation. These are equally portrayed as qualifications, or conditions for salvation. Where belief and repentance are necessary for salvation, it seems baptism is also necessary for salvation. That is the lesson of Jesus' words to Nicodemus.

Relative Necessity

Jack Cottrell, in answer to the question: *Is baptism essential for salvation?* wrote, "My straightforward (but qualified) answer is this: "Under normal circumstances, since the Day of Pentecost, YES…Water baptism is clearly described as the time or occasion during which God bestows salvation upon the one being baptized. Honest exegesis can yield no other conclusion."[86]

The lesson of John 3 is powerful, but it must also be considered relative. In what sense is it relative? To begin with, for those who lived and died under the Abrahamic covenant of the Old Testament, baptism in Jesus' name was unknown. Consequently, no such tenet was given, notwithstanding the baptism offered by John. Baptism in Jesus' name was not introduced until Jesus spoke the Great Commission, and then only to the disciples. It was not introduced to the general public until Pentecost, as Cottrell has noted. This principle would have applied to the thief on the cross (Luke 23: 39-43) and others who died prior to Pentecost. Therefore, *ean me* in John 3 must be considered relative to the time the statement was made, but there are other biblical considerations that seem to qualify Jesus' statement.

Like every passage of Scripture, the teaching of the text must be weighed against the balance of biblical instruction where salvation is concerned. For instance, it is true that one must be born of water and the Spirit in order to enter the kingdom, but baptism is not merely a matter of being plunged into and lifted from the water. Absent faith and

---

[86] Cottrell, Jack, *Is Baptism Essential for Salvation?*, http://jackcottrell.com/notes/is-baptism-essential-for-salvation/, Accessed January 10, 2018

repentance, the act is meaningless. Without faith and repentance, immersion in water is not baptism. It stands to reason, then, that where faith and repentance are not possible, the same must be true of baptism. Conversely, those who have access to biblical instruction and the capacity to understand it will undoubtedly be held to that standard.

The innocence of children is well-expressed in the pages of Scripture. Infants are the epitome of innocence. While some teach a doctrine known as *original sin*, there is no biblical reason to believe that infants are not completely free from the guilt of sin (cf. Romans 5: 18). They also lack the capacity to 1) believe in Jesus as the Son of God and 2) repent of their sins, though the absence of sin would alleviate the need. Indeed, Jesus stated that men are to become like children, replicating their state of innocence (Matthew 18: 3).

It can rightfully be inferred from Scripture that baptism as a matter of entrance into the kingdom would not apply to those too young to fulfill the requisites of belief (Mark 16: 16; John 8: 24) and repentance (Acts 2: 38; Luke 3: 3) that qualify one for baptism, notwithstanding Jesus' words to Nicodemus (John 3: 5). Wayne Jackson explains this point effectively in an article in the Christian Courier. His words would certainly apply to those too young to decide to follow Christ.

> No one is amenable to the gospel of Christ who is **incapable** of assuming the responsibilities connected with conversion. Jesus taught that those who wish to follow him must be willing to separate from loved ones—even parents—if necessary. He must be daring enough to forfeit his own life if it should come to that (Mt. 10:37; Lk. 14:26; Rev. 2:10).[87]

There are also those who have died not having had the opportunity to hear of Jesus. Consequently, they would not have the opportunity to believe in him or confess their sins. Still, Scripture states "…that they are without excuse" (Romans 1: 20) since the evidence of God surrounds them. Paul explained to the church in Rome that nature itself displays evidence of God's presence and that it is accompanied by a sense of morality and righteousness that is inherently known by men (Romans 2: 14-15). These will certainly be held accountable for their righteousness or lack of righteousness – for whether or not they sought to honor God (Romans 1: 21) – but it stands to reason that they will not be held accountable for biblical teaching about things like baptism of

---

[87] Jackson, Wayne, *What About Baptism of Young Children*, https://www.christiancourier.com/articles/499-what-about-the-baptism-of-young-children, accessed July 19, 2018.

which they have no knowledge. This is a reflection of the principle that, where it is possible to follow biblical instruction, men will be held to that standard.

While these exceptions are biblically derived based on apostolic instruction about repentance and faith, Scripture offers no *list* of baptismal exclusions. Biblically speaking, in the church age immersion in water in Jesus' name (or in the name of the Father, the Son, and the Holy Spirit) is defined as the moment of forgiveness for that person who wishes to accept Jesus as savior (Acts 2: 38; 22: 16). It is the time one becomes clothed with Christ (Galatians 3: 27) and experiences salvation (1 Peter 3: 21). Where believers are concerned, submission to baptism is expected of every man and woman.

Just as Jesus said in plainspoken fashion that people must believe and repent in order to know salvation, he has made it clear that "...unless one is born of water and the Spirit he cannot enter into the kingdom of God." (John 3: 5). It has been demonstrated here that *born of water and the Spirit* speaks to immersion in water in Jesus' name. Consequently, it is reasonable to believe that people will be held accountable to these words. They will be held accountable for baptism.

Where God's plan of salvation is concerned, grace is dependent on and subordinate to Christ, who is Lord. Absent Christ's sacrifice, mankind would not know God's grace. His sacrifice is the means by which his grace has been made available. In like manner, faith is reliant upon and subordinate to grace since, absent grace, no amount of faith could reconcile men to God. Similarly, repentance and baptism depend on and are subordinate to faith since neither one can occur independent of faith, making faith primary where one's response to the gospel message is concerned. This, however, does not mean that baptism and repentance are less important than faith any more than faith is less important than grace where redemption is concerned. According to Scripture, each has a vital role in the plan of salvation.

Salvation is by grace through faith (Ephesians 2: 8). How can this be reconciled with Jesus' portrayal of baptism in his words to Nicodemus? Baptism is simply that instrument of surrender designed by God in combination with repentance, all within the framework of faith, when one is cleansed by the blood of Christ, reborn through the work of the Holy Spirit, and receives the promised gift (presence) of the Holy Spirit. It is the water of the new birth through which one enters the kingdom of God (John 3: 5).

Baptism is presented as the biblically prescribed time at which men and women are admitted into the kingdom of God. Among those who will enter the kingdom, if there are exceptions to baptism in the church age, they are exceptions that God alone can decide. It is not up to men to nullify Jesus' words. The lesson of Scripture is that baptism is a unique unifying element in the kingdom of God (Ephesians 4: 5) and an "...elementary teaching about the Christ" (Hebrews 6: 1-2). The apostles never entertained the idea that baptism was a sign of salvation or a work of merit (a means of earning salvation). Instead, baptism is portrayed as one's expected faithful response to the gospel message.

Righteousness and Grace

God has reserved for himself, or more specifically for the Son, the judgment of people on an individual basis (John 5: 22). He has also provided guidelines by which he will judge those who seek to enter his kingdom. Salvation is by grace (Ephesians 2: 8), but men will be judged according to works (Revelation 20: 12).

Jehovah is a loving, graceful, and merciful God. He is also a forgiving God. This forgiving character is highlighted by the Apostle John when writing about the relationship between God and the believer who has sin in his life.

> [8] If we say that we have no sin, we are deceiving ourselves and the truth is not in us. [9] If we confess our sins, He is faithful and righteous to forgive us our sins and to cleanse us from all unrighteousness. (1 John 1: 8-9)

God is graceful and merciful, but he is also holy and righteous. His character traits of grace and mercy both complement and challenge his holiness and righteousness. Men are saved through grace and mercy despite the fact that mankind is unrighteous and unholy. God accepts the faithful as holy and righteous only because they have been cleansed by the blood of Christ. However, God's righteousness demands that he must be true. This is reflected in some of Jesus' closing comments in the Sermon on the Mount.

> [21] Not everyone who says to Me, 'Lord, Lord,' will enter the kingdom of heaven, but he who does the will of My Father who is in heaven *will enter*. [22] Many will say to Me on that day, 'Lord, Lord, did we not prophesy in Your name, and in Your name cast out demons, and in Your name perform many miracles?' [23] And then I will declare to them, 'I never knew you; DEPART FROM ME, YOU WHO PRACTICE LAWLESSNESS.' (Matthew 7: 21-23)

Believing/calling on his name is not sufficient to attain salvation and enter the kingdom. Only those who do the will of the Father will enter heaven. God has established conditions for acceptance into his kingdom. Doing the will of God...obeying his commands...does not earn salvation for anyone. On the other hand, one cannot enter heaven absent obedience. This is the lesson of Scripture. R. C. Foster wrote concerning these verses:

> "The dramatic ending of this sermon is the vivid picture of a great house falling with a mighty crash amid the howling elements and the raging relentless floods. It predicts the fate of the foolish man who 'heareth these words of mine, and doeth them not.'"[88]

What is most fascinating is that much of mankind seems to approach John 3 in cavalier fashion, as though what Jesus told Nicodemus is inconsequential – unrelated to one's salvation. Most are willing to accept any meaning for the term *born of water* as long as it does not involve baptism, suggesting that Jesus was being ambiguous – an ambiguity that did not surface until the sixteenth century.

If it is not possible to be confident of the meaning of Jesus' words, it is not possible to be confident in God's plan of salvation since no one can know how to be born of water and the Spirit. Men can only speculate. Yet, there is no uncertainty here. It is not in Jesus' character to teach that something is critical to salvation and leave men guessing as to what it might be. With the words *born of water and the Spirit*, he painted for Nicodemus and for all mankind an inspiring picture that is the very imagery of baptism. This is a truth of which the Early Church Fathers were fully aware and why they understood that, without question, Jesus was speaking of immersion in water.

When Jesus said, "...unless you repent, you will all likewise perish" (Luke 13: 3), he placed the responsibility to repent upon those listeners who did not want to *likewise perish*. When he said "...unless you believe that I am *He*, you will die in your sins" (John 8: 24), he placed the responsibility of belief on the shoulders of those who did not wish to *die in their sins*. In like manner, with the words, "...unless one is born of water and the Spirit he cannot enter into the kingdom of God" (John 3: 5), he had in view human responsibility. Just as people must choose to believe and repent, each one must choose to be *born of water and the Spirit* – that is, be baptized in Jesus' name.

---

[88] Foster, R. C., *Studies in the Life of Christ*, College Press Publishing Company, Joplin, MO, 1995, p. 487.

Appendix A

The following verses, when read in the KJV, demonstrate a literary device used primarily in the KJV and its derivatives as a matter of emphasis. For instance, the first verse mentioned here comes from the well-known Olivet Discourse. In his statement, Jesus notes the nearness of some of the events he was discussing. In the KJV, the writers chose to add emphasis to his statement by inserting the word *even*.

While the approach may have been effective, the reality is that the word *even* has been added to the text. It has not been translated from the original language. Many believe and teach that this represents a translation of the Greek word *kai*, but that word is not present in any of these verses. For this reason, the word *even* is missing from these same verses in other English translations; and where it is found, the writers seem to have taken their cue from the 1599 Geneva Bible and the KJV.

Matthew 24: 33	Mark 13: 29	Mark 14: 30
Mark 14: 54	John 1: 12	John 3: 13
John 5: 45	John 8: 41	John 14: 16-17
John 15: 26	Acts 2: 3	Acts 5: 37
Acts 9: 17	Acts 10: 41	Romans 1: 20
Romans 3: 21-22	Romans 4: 17	Romans 7: 4
Romans 9: 10	Romans 10: 8	1 Corinthians 2: 7
1 Corinthians 3: 1	2 Corinthians 1: 19	2 Corinthians 13: 9
Galatians 4: 14	Galatians 5: 14	Ephesians 1: 10
Ephesians 2: 15	Colossians 1: 14	Colossians 1: 25-26
1 Thess. 1: 10	1 Thess. 4: 3	2 Thess. 2: 8-9
1 Timothy 6: 3	2 Timothy 2: 9	Titus 1: 12
Hebrews 1: 9	Hebrews 5: 14	Hebrews 6: 20
James 4: 1	1 Peter 1: 9	1 Peter 3: 4
1 Peter 3: 21	1 John 2: 25	1 John 5: 4
1 John 5: 6	1 John 5: 20	

Bibliography

Aphrahat, *The Demonstrations*, Treatises, 6: 14: 4. Aphrahat, *The Demonstrations*, https://www.catholic.com/tract/baptismal-grace, accessed October 10, 2017

Barnabas, *The Epistle of Barnabas* 11: 1, Early Christian Writings, http://www.earlychristianwritings.com/text/barnabas-hoole.html, accessed August 30, 2017.

Barnabas, *The Epistle of Barnabas* 11: 8 & 11, Early Christian Writings http://www.earlychristianwritings.com/text/barnabas-hoole.html, accessed August 30, 2017.

Basil the Great, *On the Holy Spirit*, Myriobiblos, http://www.myriobiblos.gr/texts/english/basil_spiritu_12.html, accessed September 5, 2017.

Beasely-Murray, G. R., *Baptism in the New Testament*, William B. Eerdman's Publishing Company, Grand Rapids, MI., 1973.

Benson, Joseph, *Joseph Benson's Commentary of the Old and New Testaments*, studylight.org, https://www.studylight.org/commentaries/rbc/ephesians-5.html, accessed August 8, 2017.

Bently, R. K., *John 3: 5 – What Does it Mean to be, "Born of Water?"* http://rkbentley.blogspot.com/2008/11/john-35-what-does-it-mean-to-be-born-of.html, accessed August 1, 2017.

Boice, James, Wood, A. Skevington, *The Expositor's Bible Commentary with the New International Version*, Zondervan Publishing House, Grand Rapids, MI, 1995.

Bromiley, G. W. editor and translator. *'Of Baptism,' in Zwingli and Bullinger, 'Library of Christian Classic" Ichthus Editions,* The Westminster Press, Philadelphia, PA.

Bruce, F. F., General Editor, *New International Bible Commentary*, Zondervan Publishing, Grand Rapids, MI, 1979.

Bullinger, E. W., *E. W. Bullinger's Companion Bible Notes*, studylight.org, https://www.studylight.org/commentaries/bul/john-3.html, accessed August 15, 2017.

Calvin, John, *Calvin's Commentaries*, biblehub.com, http://biblehub.com/commentaries/calvin/john/3.htm, accessed July 22, 2017.

Calvin, John, *Calvin's Commentary on the Bible*, studylight.org, https://www.studylight.org/commentaries/cal/ephesians-5.html, accessed August 18, 2017.

Calvin, John, *Institutes of the Christian Religion*, Hendrickson Publishers, Book Fourth, Peabody, MA, 2008.

Campbell, Alexander, *The Christian System*, Gospel Advocate Company, Nashville, TN, 2001.

Carson, D. A., *Carson on the meaning of "born of water and of the Spirit"* https://aaronshaf.wordpress.com/2011/12/21/d-a-carson-on-the-meaning-of-born-of-water-and-of-the-spirit/, accessed August 23, 2017.

Chrysostom, John, *Homilies on Second Corinthians*, 390 AD, https://biblehub.com/commentaries/chrysostom/2_corinthians/3.htm, accessed October 17, 2017.

Coffman, John, *Coffman's Commentaries on the Bible - John*, A.C.U Press, Abilene, TX, 1974.

Coffman, James B., *James Burton Coffman Commentaries: 1&2 Thessalonians, 1&2 Timothy, Titus, and Philemon*, ACU Press, Abilene, TX, 1986, p. 86.

Coke, Thomas, *Thomas Coke Commentary on the Holy Bible*, https://www.studylight.org/commentaries/tcc/luke-2.html, accessed April 26, 2018.

Constable, Thomas, *Expository Notes of Dr. Thomas Constable*, studylight.org https://www.studylight.org/commentaries/dcc/john-3.html, accessed June 15, 2017.

Cottrell, Jack, *Baptism A Biblical Study*, College Press Publishing, Jopplin, MO, 1989.

Cottrell, Jack, *Is Baptism Essential for Salvation?*, http://jackcottrell.com/notes/is-baptism-essential-for-salvation/, accessed January 10, 2018

Cottrell, Jack, *What Is the Meaning of the "Baptism in Fire" in Matthew 3:11?* http://jackcottrell.com/notes/what-is-the-meaning-of-the-baptism-in-fire-in-matthew-311/, accessed April 27, 2018.

Cyprian, *The Epistles of Cyprian*, http://www.sacred-texts.com/chr/ecf/005/0050098.htm, accessed September 30, 2017.

Cyril of Jerusalem, 348AD, *"On Baptism,"*
http://www.bebaptized.org/UndeniableFacts.htm,
accessed October 12, 2017.

Cyril of Jerusalem, *Catechetical Lectures*, Cyril of Jerusalem, *Catechetical Lectures*, http://www.bebaptized.org/UndeniableFacts.htm, accessed October 12, 2017.

Darby, John, *Darby's Synopsis of the New Testament*, studylight.org, https://www.studylight.org/commentaries/dsn/john-3.html, accessed July 14, 2017.

Ellicott, Charles, *Ellicott's Commentary for English Readers*, studylight.org, https://www.studylight.org/commentaries/ebc/ephesians-5.html, accessed August 25, 2017.

Ferguson, Everett, *Baptism in the Early Church*, citing Clement of Rome, William B. Eerdman Publishing Company, Grand Rapids, MI, 2009.

Foster, R. C., *Studies in the Life of Christ*, College Press Publishing Company, Joplin, MO., 1995.

Frutchenbaum, Arnold G., *The Eight Covenants of the Bible*
http://www.messianicassociation.org/ezine17-af.covenants.htm
accessed January 20, 2018.

Gill, John, *Gill's Exposition of the Entire Bible*, biblehub.com
http://biblehub.com/john/3.htm, accessed August 15, 2017.

Gill, John, *Gill's Exposition of the Entire Bible*, biblehub.com
http://biblehub.com/john/3-5.htm, accessed August 22, 2017.

Gill, John, *Gill's Exposition of the Entire Bible*, biblehub.com
http://biblehub.com/mark/1-4.htm, accessed August 10, 2017.

Gill, John, *Gill's Exposition of the Entire Bible*, biblehub.com
http://biblehub.com/commentaries/gill/1_john/5.htm,
accessed August 15, 2017.

Helwys, Thomas, & Richard Groves (Ed.). *The Mystery of Iniquity. Book 1.* Mercer University Press, 1998

Hermas, *Shepherd of Hermas*, Early Christian Writings, http://www.earlychristianwritings.com/text/shepherd-lightfoot.html, accessed August 30, 2017.

Hurte, William, *The Restoration New Testament Commentary in Question and Answer Form: A Catechetical Commentary*, Old Paths Publishing Company, Rosemead, CA, 1964

Ignatius, *Epistle of Ignatius to the Trallians,* Chapter II, Early Christian Writings, http://www.earlychristianwritings.com/text/ignatius-trallians-longer.html, accessed August 28, 2017.

Irenaeus, *Against Heresies*, bk. 1, chap. 21, sec. 1, http://www.earlychristianwritings.com/text/irenaeus-book1.html, accessed September 10, 2017.

Irenaeus, *Fragments From Lost Writings, No. 34*, Irenaeus, *Fragments From Lost Writings, No. 34*, http://www.newadvent.org/fathers/0134.htm, accessed September 3, 2017.

Jackson, Wayne, *What About Baptism of Young Children,* https://www.christiancourier.com/articles/499-what-about-the-baptism-of-young-children, accessed July 19, 2018.

Jamieson, Robert, A. R. Fausset, David Brown, *Commentary Critical and Explanatory on the Whole Bible*, https://www.studylight.org/commentaries/jfb/ephesians-5.html, accessed August 25, 2017.

Kostenberger, Andreas, J., *Zondervan Illustrated Biblical Backgrounds Commentary, Volume 2*, Zondervan Publishing, Grand Rapids, MI 1984.

Lange, Johanne, L*ange's Commentary on the Holy Scriptures: Critical, Doctrinal, and Homiletical*, https://www.studylight.org/commentaries/lcc/john-3.html, accessed July 22, 2017.

Lange, Johanne, L*ange's Commentary on the Holy Scriptures: Critical, Doctrinal, and Homiletical,* https://www.studylight.org/commentaries/lcc/ephesians-5.html,accessed August 21, 2017.

Liberman, Mark, *What does "even" even mean?* http://languagelog.ldc.upenn.edu/nll/?p=2943, accessed August 12, 2017.

Lockhart, Clinton. *Principles of Interpretation Revised Edition*, Gospel Light Publishing Company, Delight, AR.

Luther, Martin, *Martin Luther's Commentary*, https://www.stepbible.org/?q=version=Luther|reference=Joh.3 accessed August 19, 2018

Luther, Martin. *The Necessity of Baptism*, http://www.catholic.com/tracts/the-necessity-of-baptism, accessed August 20, 2018.

MacArthur, John, *The MacArthur New Testament Commentary*, https://www.gty.org/library/bibleqnas-library/QA0302/what-does-it-mean-to-be-born-of-water-and-spirit, Accessed February 19, 2018.

MacDonald, William, *Believer's Bible Commentary*, Thomas Nelson Publishers, Nashville, Atlanta, London, Vancouver, 1995.

Martyr, Justin, *First Apology*, http://www.newadvent.org/fathers/0126.htm., accessed September 23, 2017.

Martyr, Justin, *Constitutions of the Holy Apostles*, Martyr, Justin, *Constitutions of the Holy Apostles*, http://www.bible.ca/H-baptism.htm, accessed September 23, 2017.

Martyr, Justin, *Constitutions of the Holy Apostles*, www.bebaptized.org/UndeniableFacts.htm, accessed October 25, 2017.

McPherson, Joseph D., *BORN OF WATER, BORN OF THE SPIRIT - What Did Jesus Mean by Being "Born of Water?"* http://www.fwponline.cc/v16n1/v16n1joemac.html, accessed July 23, 2017.

Natureofwriting.com/conjunctive-adverbs/, accessed December 27, 2018

Nazianz, Gregory, Oration on Holy Baptism https://biblehub.com/library/cyril/lectures_of_s_cyril_of_jerusalem/oration_xl_the_oration_on.htm, accessed October 10, 2017

Neighbour, Robert, *The Wells of Living Water Commentary*, studylight.org, https://www.studylight.org/commentaries/lwc/john-3.html, accessed July 3, 2017.

NTgreek.org/learn_nt_greek/classify-genitive.htm, accessed December 16, 2018

Robertson, A. T., *Robertson's Word Pictures of the New Testament*, studylight.org, https://www.studylight.org/commentaries/rwp/john-3.html, accessed July 15, 2017.

Robertson, A. T., *Robertson's Word Pictures of the New Testament*, studylight.org, https://www.studylight.org/commentaries/rwp/matthew-26.html, accessed August 12, 2017.

Robertson, A. T., *Robertson's Word Pictures of the New Testament*, studylight.org, https://www.studylight.org/commentaries/rwp/acts-2.html, accessed August 12, 2017.

Smith, Chuck, *Chuck Smith Bible Commentary*, studylight.org https://www.studylight.org/commentaries/csc/john-3.html, accessed July 5, 2017.

Spurgeon, Charles Haddon, , Susannah Spurgeon, Joseph Harrald, , *The Autobiography of Charles H. Spurgeon*, Vol. 1, F.H. Revell, Chicago: 1898.

Tertullian, *On Baptism*, Early Christian Writings, http://www.earlychristianwritings.com/text/tertullian21.html, Accessed August 28, 2017.

Wenham, G. J., J. A. Motyer, D. A. Carson, R. T. France, editors, *New Bible Commentary*, Inter-Varsity Press, Nottingham, England, 1994.

Williamson, Darrel T., *Erasmus of Rotterdam's Influence upon Anabaptism: The Case of Belthasr Hubmaier*, Simon Frasier University, 2005.

Writingexplained.org/grammar-dictionary/genitive case, accessed June 28, 2017.